# TRANSFORMATIONAL PSYCHOTHERAPY

# TRANSFORMATIONAL PSYCHOTHERAPY

## AN APPROACH TO CREATIVE HYPNOTIC COMMUNICATION

Arthur Phillips, M.D.
Department of Psychiatry
Cornell University Medical College
New York, New York

ELSEVIER • NEW YORK
New York • Oxford

Elsevier North Holland, Inc.
52 Vanderbilt Avenue, New York, New York 10017

Sole distributors outside the United States and Canada:

Elsevier Science Publishers B.V.
P.O. Box 211, 1000 AE Amsterdam, The Netherlands



Library of Congress Cataloging in Publication Data

Phillips, Arthur.
Transformational psychotherapy: an approach to creative hypnotic communication
Includes index.
1. Psychotherapy. I. Title [DNLM: 1. Psychotherapy. WM 420 P557t]
RC480.5.P48 616.89'14 81-5518
ISBN 0-444-00652-4 AACR2

*Copy Editor* Lola Peters
*Desk Editor* John Hawes
*Design* Edmée Froment
*Design Editor* Glen Burris
*Cover Design* Paul Agule Design
*Production Manager* Joanne Jay
*Compositor* J.M. Post Graphics
*Printer* Haddon Craftsmen

Manufactured in the United States of America

*To our children,*
*Eric and Amy*

# CONTENTS

# PREFACE

Over the past decade, particularly in the wake of the human potential movement in the United States, a large number of diverse disciplines have entered the arena of American and Western European psychology. Although some of the techniques employed in these disciplines are thought of as "new," many have actually emerged as modern variations of ancient techniques.

These methods have a number of things in common. First, they are extremely powerful psychologically and are therefore impressive to both psychotherapists and laymen. Second, since many of these techniques (hypnosis, altered states of consciousness, neurolinguistic programming, psychodrama, etc.) are not included as an integral part of the clinical psychology and psychiatry programs in the United States, the responsible practitioner of psychotherapy simply has no adequate set of guidelines in which to place these divergent modalities.

As a result, without a workable frame of reference for the practitioner, there are powerful and effective methods available to the profession that are just not being utilized.

This volume is intended to provide such a frame of reference. It can be considered to have come from a synthesis of mainstream psychotherapy as currently practiced in the United States and certain disciplines that make their appearance as isolated schools of thought. This apparent isolation or fragmentation is a by-product of history and geography. Given a proper perspective, the fields of psychoanalysis, psychopharmacology, hypnosis, psychodrama, altered states of consciousness, behaviorism, neurolinguistic programming, humanistic psychology, and philosophy become compatible resources for the practitioner, to be employed with skill, judgment, and grace.

A few years ago the climate was more of a contest between many factions for primacy or acceptability. Currently, there seems to be a climate of respect and interest in all of these areas, and we are searching for common denominators as well as some overall useful and practical guiding principles.

This volume is an outgrowth of my work with these issues in a psychotherapeutic outpatient setting. A useful approach has in fact emerged that is applicable on many levels. Most important of all is that it is an open-ended model that emphasizes continued expansion. This allows one to include whatever is useful, new or old.

This book is appropriate for psychotherapists, teachers of psychotherapists, and advanced students of psychotherapy.

The scope of this volume covers two main areas. Under the rubric of what will be described as "Transformational Psychotherapy," Part I outlines the preparatory skills necessary to do such therapy. Part II outlines a format for the therapy itself.

With respect to Part I, covering preparatory skills, information is presented to indicate the minimum level of competency necessary to perform each skill. For thorough and detailed instruction, key references are offered throughout. Mastering the minimum level enables one to move on to utilization levels as soon as possible.

Because the scope of this volume is wide enough to embrace the variety of fields under discussion, the depth of treatment of any individual topic is limited. Only that amount of technique and theory necessary for the reader to understand the conceptual framework on which the book is based is included. Naturally, for the study of any of the topics in great depth, the reader is referred to the current literature in the given subspecialty.

Part II deals with transformational psychotherapy itself. Principles are presented and are illustrated from time to time with clinical examples. The attempt has been made to frame the presentation in a manner that encourages the reader to develop an individual style rather than to act in strict adherence to some doctrine.

There are many books already available on the various topics touched upon within this work. What is truly unique about this book is the presentation of a workable structure enabling these different disciplines to be held in a coherent and effective manner.

If successful, this offers a conceptual bridge to an entirely new and relatively unexplored dimension of psychotherapeutic endeavor.

The time of a new frontier has always been a very special and exciting time. We are truly fortunate.

# ACKNOWLEDGMENTS

I am deeply grateful to my wife, Madalyn Phillips, for the dialogue that helped me clarify points along the way, for her careful reading of the manuscript, and for her invaluable suggestions regarding style as well as content.

I wish to acknowledge Steve Hymowitz, Michael Bennahum, and Susan Rudnick for the supportive feedback and fertile arena necessary for constructive energy and the growth of ideas. I want to thank Matt Fried for insisting that I publish my work and for contributing the concepts of both a temporal dimension and a multipattern objection scan in the ecological check of reframing. I also want to thank Star Pack's Bob Nowicki for his great assistance in the typing and preparation of the manuscript.

Finally, I wish to extend my gratitude to all of my patients and all of my clients for teaching me what I need to know.

# INTRODUCTION

By way of orientation, it would be useful to understand the distinct emphasis I place on health and well-being, as opposed to the traditional emphasis on psychopathology in psychotherapy.

Although our field is officially dedicated to promoting mental *health*, the reality is that the training and the practice of psychotherapy in the United States is primarily the field of working with mental *illness*, rather than mental health. This distinction is essential to an appreciation of this work.

Of course, the practicing psychotherapist must learn about psychopathology and its mechanisms. If, however, psychopathology is the only thing learned, with the assumption that once you clear it up health automatically ensues, and that you need not know much about health itself, a disservice is done to both the therapist and the client.

When one is trained basically as a psychopathologist, then as soon as the pathology disappears, the professional relationship between therapist and client is terminated.

When we shift the basic frame of reference of the work we do from pathology to health, the study of psychopathology does not disappear from the curriculum. On the contrary, the understanding of psychopathology remains absolutely necessary—but it is no longer sufficient. For the mental *health* practitioner the purpose of knowing about psychopathology is to clear it up as quickly as possible and then move on to the business of mental *health*.

The notion that health is merely the absence of sickness is naive. Actually, it is no less absurd than the claim that a person who is not sick is as healthy as an olympic athlete, a prima ballerina, or a championship gymnast.

There are ranges of health. There are degrees of health. Therefore, if we become mental health practitioners as opposed to mental illness practitioners we must continue to learn about psychopathology and its treatment in a setting in which we are fundamentally learning about health and well-being.

Learning about health and well-being is a study that never ends. It is continually expanding. The more we live, the more we learn; the more we look, the more we see; the more we experience, the more we develop and grow. A definition of health would necessarily include the concepts of continuing expansion, continuing realization, continuing enlightenment, into areas of continuing unknown and frontier.

It is only the study of illness that has a discrete ending, that is, when the disease is cured and there is no more pathology. That ending constitutes the beginning of health, and health continues, and grows, and expands.

The transformational psychotherapist is primarily interested in the client's well-being, development, growth, and continuing enlightenment.

With that frame of mind we can proceed with a certain sense of direction.

The principles of transformational psychotherapy are simple and easy to understand. Therefore, the real emphasis will be on putting these principles into effective action. This requires certain operational skills on the part of the practitioner. The first part of this book will be devoted to outlining the necessary preparatory operational skills required to implement the strategy or strategies of a transformational psychotherapy.

The prerequisite areas of skills development for transformational psychotherapy involve the following:

1. Diagnosis and treatment
2. Rapport
3. Hypnosis and hypnotic communication
4. Key operational components
5. Appreciation of context
6. Personal development of the therapist

Obviously, the development of each of the above six areas can continue through life, having no true end point. This assertion is not meant to be discouraging, but, quite the contrary, it should open up the gratifying vista that reveals us continuing to perfect our skills, continuing to develop, and becoming increasingly masterful. Furthermore, even though these skills can be endlessly perfected, it is important for the reader to realize that there is a certain minimum level of practice and of proficiency that can be reached in all of the above six areas so that transformational psychotherapy can be adequately performed.

Part I outlines and elucidates what that minimum requirement would be, and also opens the areas of further development for the serious student and practitioner. The minimum basic level is readily acquired, as long as we truly desire to develop our skills in this area. When that minimum level is reached, the combining of these six ingredients is extremely rewarding, and that is the subject of Part II.

Although Part I is written in a linear fashion, meaning that one unit follows another unit following another unit, it is to be understood that these units are actually not a sequence, but are six ingredients; all the same, the printed word requires a linear presentation. The truth is one can enter into simultaneous study of all of these six areas. In fact, the simultaneous development of these six areas is *encouraged*.

It is further recommended that the reader read through the entire first section on preparatory skills before embarking seriously on the in-depth study of any of the topics. By so doing, a certain inner understanding and integration of the relationship of these areas will begin to form within the reader's own mind. The result will be that the intuition of the reader will lead to appropriate "next steps" for training and in-depth study available elsewhere in the literature and in classes and workshops throughout the community.

PART

# I

# PREPARATORY SKILLS

CHAPTER

# 1

# DIAGNOSIS AND TREATMENT

## TRANSFORMATION

The difference between transformation and ordinary change is profound. Ordinary change usually signifies a partial revision. Transformation signifies an essential change of the whole rather than of a part. In other words, transformation is a total change of form. This can mean a change in the very nature of something.

There is nothing new or unusual about transformation as a phenomenon or as a subject of discussion. It is an integral part of the nature and evolution of this planet. In fact we have all witnessed transformation as so much a common part of everyday experience that it frequently goes unnoticed. In the literature the examples of transformation often chosen for illustration owe their clarity to an emphasis on obvious physical change, for example, the caterpillar becoming the butterfly, the tadpole becoming the frog, the microscopic one-celled animal becoming the newborn baby.

In addition to the physical dimension, human beings also have access to the nonphysical dimension—the abstract, the mental, the psychological. Transformation occurs in this realm as well. It is especially observable whenever there has been a transformation of personality. Such change is often seen following developmental stages or major life events, such as puberty or the death of a parent. When we speak of transformation of a personality the change is just as profound as that of the caterpillar to the butterfly, even though the theatre of change is nonphysical.

Throughout history the capacity for such dramatic change has led people to wonder about the very nature of human beings, those creatures who apparently have the "choice" or capacity to change or not change so profoundly. Obviously the nature of such a being would have to be a greater construct than any given personality or role. Therefore, personality transformation has typically been the subject of religious and philosophical works through the centuries, works that emphasize forms and constructs larger than the obvious.

When a person makes a transformational change in his or her life, the external circumstances may or may not change. Frequently, following the change, the circumstances in the immediate environment are exactly the same as they were prior to the event. The difference is in the essence of a person's life. Identical circumstances may be experienced in a totally new way. For example, a circumstance once perceived as a great difficulty may now be perceived as a deep, exciting, personal challenge. The difference is in the experience of the circumstances rather than the circumstances themselves.

When the transformation has occurred purposefully with conscious intention attached to the event such as in a psychotherapy, rather than passively, by accident, or simply as a part of a developmental stage, there can be an additional dimension to the event. Once people realize that they are able to alter the quality of their experience of personal reality, that such power is available to them and is indeed their birthright, the entire game of life begins to be played on a totally new level. A new choice enters the game.

When a new problem is encountered one can either enter the process that this problem initially implies, or recontextualize the "problem" as a "challenge" and engage in the new process that this "challenge" implies. Life becomes an education and an engaging process. In current mainstream psychotherapy such an outcome would be a very fortunate by-product. In a transformational psychotherapy this kind of outcome is one of the central goals.

## TRANSFORMATIONAL PSYCHOTHERAPY

The term *transformational psychotherapy* is being used here in a functional sense. It means literally the form of psychotherapy that effects or produces a transformation. There is a future dimension as well. When effective, transformational psychotherapy assists a person to move successively to the next areas in which personal evolution takes place, that is, a progressive spiral of expanding areas of personal evolution that, when actualized successfully, is self-generating and does not require continuing interaction between therapist and client into the future.

Transformational psychotherapy can be distinguished from other functional terms, for example, supportive therapy and insight oriented psychotherapy. These terms have areas in which they overlap. It is possible during an insight oriented psychotherapy to receive support. It is possible during a supportive psychotherapy to have insight. It is possible during either of those therapies for a transformation to take place in an individual.

It is equally important to note, however, that it is possible during an insight oriented therapy for a great deal of insight and support to be achieved without transformation. During supportive psychotherapy immense support may be experienced without insight or transformation. Therefore, "transformational psychotherapy" is a useful term. It should be applied to those forms of psychotherapy, new or old, that are directed toward and are considered successful when a personal transformation in the client has been achieved.

I have one further comment on the use of this term. Psychoanalysis, for instance, can produce personal education, personal transformation, or both. Yet, I would apply the term transformational psychotherapy to psychoanalysis only *when* it is producing personal transformation as a goal; I would not apply that term to the generic psychoanalysis at all times and under all circumstances. I would definitely not use the term for psychoanalysis when it is primarily an educational tool.

The need for such a term as transformational psychotherapy has emerged since a number of sophisticated and powerful techniques have begun to reenter the psychiatric, psychological armamentarium. These techniques enable practitioners to approach personality transformation directly, rather than discover it as a fortunate by-product of a given treatment modality. Like any other term describing a treatment in terms of its goal rather than its method, it then can be considered a treatment of choice under appropriate circumstances.

In the mind of the practitioner of transformational psychotherapy there is also a different frame of reference with regard to the therapeutic process itself. In mainstream psychotherapies there are regularly scheduled meetings during which therapists understand that they are engaged in an ongoing process where the sessions are designed to move their clients further and further in the desired direction. The therapy may extend over a few years, and there is a sense that the ongoing sessions are necessary to effect the change. In a transformational psychotherapy the change is performed at a deeper level as soon as possible, perhaps at the very outset. If one were to categorize, in one single thought, the frame of reference of the transformational psychotherapist while working, it would be, "Do it all. Right now."

This is not to imply that a transformational psychotherapy actually takes place solely in an instant and requires no evaluation, no follow-up, and no process. On the contrary, evaluation is necessary; change unfolds over quite a bit of time, requiring responsible follow-up. The formula of "Do it all. Right now" implies something else.

It is possible to mentally recontextualize the process of life in such a manner that the events of life and the circumstances of life are experienced in a totally different way than prior to the recontextualization. The psychological time involved could be instantaneous, even during a single session. (A more detailed discussion of this subject is in Chapters 4–9.) The sort of outcome of such a mental event is the later unfolding through time of the changes during the transformational psychotherapeutic session.

To "do it all, right now" implies parameters of reality that are not in the tangible time/space parameters of the physical universe as we usually think of it. It is possible to engage in a process in which something is "all" done in an instant *in psychological time,* rather than in actual physical time. This is one of the cornerstones of transformational psychotherapeutic technique. By the utilization of psychological time in which very large things can be created and/or canceled in an instant, in essence, on the blueprint level of the process, it is possible to effect deep and inclusive *internal* change rapidly.

Therefore, a unique aspect of transformational psychotherapy is that in the work sessions the emphasis is on revision of the structure of reality that cohesively produces the original negative picture. The follow-up sessions are typically the sharing of experience, the content of life, the progress resulting from the "work sessions."

In practice work sessions and follow-up sessions might not be purely marked out as separate sessions, and a given session with the client may have elements of both. In my office practice it has not been uncommon to notice with certain clients that a single comprehensive session lasting approximately five hours resulted in sufficiently profound internal change manifesting over time so that follow-up sessions two months later, six months later, and again two years later showed results at least equal to those I usually found using traditional methods with frequent regular sessions over similar periods of time, if not even longer periods of time.

It must be emphasized at this point that it is true that *things do take time*. That is true. The question is, what takes time and what does not? Profound internal personal change can occur in an instant. The engineering of such instances, the facilitation of such instances, is central to transformational psychotherapy. All of those events occur within the mind and can take an instant. The *unfolding of events* occurs in the physical universe and requires time.

In effect, planting a seed can be instantaneous. For flowers to actually grow, a nurturing process is required. In mainstream psychotherapy the nurturing process requires active participation of the therapist as a coparticipant in the process itself. In a transformational psychotherapy, since the internal change includes psychological structures that unfold the process automatically like the internal genetic codes of the seeds of plants that grow in nature without requiring the assistance of a gardener, there are differences in the relationship between therapist and client. The relationship is deep and very close. The transformational psychotherapist has basically one role. It is that of guide, coach, or mentor in an atmosphere of responsibility, closeness, and determination. The utilization of the psychotherapist's office as the arena for the encounter of process is minimized, and the use of the world at large—for the unfolding of the process—is maximized.

Put in simple terms, when one is fully aware of the strategic differences between transformational psychotherapy and most mainstream psychotherapies, very large distinctions can be noted. When one is not fully aware of such strategic issues, then perhaps the only difference noted might be that a transformational psychotherapy tends to take a shorter time to achieve a similar result. Frankly, the latter observation does not adequately describe the difference. To the relatively uninformed the result may, in fact, seem similar. To the more informed the result is different by an order of magnitude.

The awarenesses in a transformation not only involve the relief of symptoms and positive experience where there was negative, but also the more profound awareness that one has within oneself, the power at any instant to transform one's experience of life itself. This carries deep implications for continuing change, continuing development, and continuing expansion of health beyond current understandings of health. In other words, it is a form of personal evolution with continued expansion into new worlds of experience.

## MATCHING CLIENT AND THERAPY

Transformational psychotherapy is not appropriate for all people at all times in their lives. Even for those for whom it is appropriate, timing is essential. The medical principle of accurate diagnosis leading to accurate choice of treatment serves us well in this situation. The principle also extends beyond the field of medicine, where it is known as "qualifying the client." Is the client appropriate for the services you have to deliver? If so, proceed. If not, refer the client elsewhere, thereby rendering an appropriate service by doing so.

The two areas to which one must pay close attention in matching the client for transformational psychotherapy are (1) internal resources and (2) the quality of the current set of circumstances in the client's life. These two areas measure the function of capacity for change, while at the same time they monitor the appropriate timing for personal transformation. The following may provide some helpful guidelines.

### Internal Resources

Most of the resources necessary for utilizing transformational psychotherapy appear to be subsumed under the rubric of capacity for sustained attention. Essentially, whatever it takes for a person to maintain concentration and attention for a relatively long period of time, that is, from one-half hour to two hours, is what is necessary for effective participation.

In other words, the ability to maintain a set, suspend that set, entertain another, suspend that set, entertain another, make choices considering these sets as parts of a whole, and considering the choice as an entity unto itself—all of these functions require concentration. In addition, it is useful for clients to be able to hold the sets on an unconscious level, as well as on a conscious level, and, although formal studies have not been done in this area, it appears clinically that hypnotizability, in the sense that Herbert Spiegel, M.D. uses it, would be very useful. Dr. Spiegel considers hypnotizability to be a highly specific measure of capacity for sustained attention—particularly on deep levels—and he has developed a test for measuring this. The test, known as the Hypnotic Induction Profile, is easily learned and can be performed in the office setting, usually taking no more than 10 minutes from beginning to end.

Naturally, the requirement of the ability to sustain attention rules out certain severe pathological states as inappropriate for transformational psychotherapy. Such states would include organic brain syndromes, severe mental retardation, certain forms of schizophrenia, and those neuroses that interfere with communication, such as severe depressive neuroses or phobic reactions when actively occurring. Of course, there are exceptions to every rule. Whatever the diagnosis, transformational psychotherapy can be considered if attention and concentration can be sustained for at least half an hour. For practical purposes, and especially for the beginner, it is recommended that this sort of therapy be attempted with individuals holding a healthy capacity for attention and concentration.

In addition to the capacity for sustained concentration and attention, the element of motivation is crucial. Clients require the motivation necessary to support and sustain them through periods of uncertainty, apparent paradox, and, if we are successful, major life changes. There are a number of methods that can assist a person to become positively motivated, whether or not they are experiencing motivation at the moment. These can be utilized during the course of therapy. It is not crucial that the person evidence motivation at the time of an initial interview; what is useful to determine, however, is the capacity for motivation if it is not in evidence, just as it is useful to determine the capacity for attention and concentration even if these qualities are not evident at the moment when one first encounters the client.

## Life Circumstances

Given the internal resources of the client and the resources of the therapist as sufficient to effect personal transformation, there is one overriding question that needs to be answered. Is a personal transformation the most sensible approach for these circumstances at this particular time in the life of the client? For example, if a light bulb burns out in one of the lamps at home, even if it were the easiest thing in the world to convert the entire home to candlelight, would it be appropriate to transform the source of illumination in the home, or would it be better to simply replace the light bulb with a new one? This illustrates the kind of problems that require decisions in the realm of clinical judgment. Many of the transformational techniques available work on such a deep level that major change in a system becomes relatively easy. Therefore, for the clinician the question becomes, "Is it a good idea to do the process?" rather than, "Can it be done?" Ultimately, it is a matter of judgment. Some of the issues to be taken into account, however, can be noted.

One of the most appropriate indications for transformation would be stagnation in personal development or in progress through life. People who find themselves either stuck in a position or constantly replaying life as though it were a tape loop would be good candidates for this process. Even if clients themselves do not perceive the problem in this manner, if the therapist can hold the problem in this frame of reference the decision can weigh heavily in favor of a transformational process.

The working hypothesis is that the client's intellect and resources have been used in the best way possible, given fundamental assumptions and beliefs about the world. The "ruts" that people find themselves in are considered to be natural consequences of those basic assumptions about life.

The rut itself is evidence of the healthy capacity of the human brain to promote stability and constancy out of overwhelmingly complicated and immeasurable amounts of data that the human nervous system constantly processes. Strange as it may seem, the rut or the stuck position is an indicator of an excellently functioning system; the "rut" is simply a matter of *what* is being held constant or stable. In the computer industry the problem is known as "garbage in, garbage out." In other words, given a poor phonograph record, an excellent phonograph will produce every pop and crackle of the poor record. This is a fault of the record, not of the system. The person in a rut or in a stuck position has an excellent "stabilizer" system. It is the negative personal programming that is being held stable and is at the heart of the matter.

Whatever the life circumstances, as long as they constitute a stuck position where all choices appear to be negative or unproductive, a transformational process may be indicated.

Transformational psychotherapy goes to the roots of assumptions and belief systems and effects change on that level.

## RESOURCES OF THE THERAPIST

We have already delineated in broad strokes some internal resources necessary for the client to have in order to anticipate a positive outcome. There is no doubt whatsoever that the client must be evaluated diagnostically to rule out those disorders and life situations that would contraindicate this form of therapy.

Let us turn our attention now to the resources of the therapist, which are twofold: personal and professional. The personal development of the psychotherapist is discussed in greater detail in Chapter 6. The following sections discuss the necessary professional skills and experiences required in transformational therapy.

### Diagnostic Skills

The question is still an open one as to whether the fundamental diagnostic phase and the subsequent treatment phase need to be carried out by the same person. Although this is not the subject of discussion in this book, it is an issue that needs to be addressed by responsible practitioners in the field. At the very least it is extremely useful for the practitioner to be able to perform both functions—diagnosis and treatment—and at the very most it may prove in time to be a requirement. It is feasible in practice to call in a diagnostician early in the process and through appropriate conference and communication to refer the case to an appropriately trained psychotherapist.

From the standpoint of diagnosis, the practitioner must be trained to be able to recognize and rule out those disorders that interfere with sustained attention span and appropriate reality testing. Although formal studies have not been done in this area, clinical experience would indicate that active psychosis, organic brain syndromes, severe depressions, and drug toxicities, to name a few, would have to be recognized and found to be inappropriate for this form of treatment. It is easier to state what diagnostic entities or states would be inappropriate for a transformational psychotherapy than to give a complete list of what conditions would be appropriate for transformational therapy. In fact, as stated earlier, there are broad principles rather than diagnostic classifications that call for a transformational psychotherapy.

The emphasis in this section is on the requisite skills of the diagnostician. The diagnostician should be able to recognize and diagnose appropriate pathological states that would make such therapy inappropriate. The ability to detect organic disease is invaluable.

Following the diagnostic phase, a fully trained psychotherapist having obtained the skills outlined in Part I of this book, and having had practice in applying them, as outlined in Part II, would be perfectly capable of conducting the subsequent transformational psychotherapy. It is primarily but not exclusively in the diagnostic or screening phase that the skills of detection of organicity and severe pathological states would be required.

Processes of the scope and extent of psychotherapy considered to be transformational cross many cultural lines. Preindustrial societies, without benefit of our technology, are very advanced in personality development. Rites of passage, tribal ceremonies, and communal support for developmental gains may be central to the survival of the group as well as the personal satisfaction of the members of the group.

One may not know how the diagnostic considerations were made in such culturally different societies. It can be assumed with reasonable conviction, however, that obvious disturbances of attention were noticed by the practitioner, if not the community, and dealt with differently. This is why it ultimately remains an open question regarding necessary training for the diagnostic phase. It is very difficult for competent psychotherapists to miss a disorder of concentration and attention even if they are not medically trained.

## Psychotherapy Skills

### *Directorial Role*

The fundamental skills that are taught during an ordinary psychotherapist's training are also necessary in the training of the transformational psychotherapist. Differentiation between external and internal phenomena is crucial. This is a typical emphasis in psychotherapeutic training and applies here as well. It is important for the psychotherapist to be able to differentiate between the client's external behavior and phenomena and his or her own internal behavior and to recognize the illusions of overlap as seen in projection and countertransference.

The psychotherapist must have the ability to be in the presence of intense affect and remain in a directorial role. Here the term "directorial" is used in the psychodramatic sense of being outside of the drama itself. In analytical terms this might be referred to as the executive functioning of the ego. To be in the presence of strong emotional issues and not be swept away by them is really the issue. The two kinds of concerns that tend to sweep one away are those that have personal relevance in the life of the practitioner and those that have universal relevance in the lives of all human beings. However done, and in whatever style, good psychotherapy training achieves this freedom in the practitioner. It is not only a question of the affect itself, it is also a question of identification with the client. It is crucial that the therapist have the ability to engage empathetically with the client and also have the ability to disengage and disassociate and to utilize information. Since the development of this ability is the core of the training of all psychotherapists, we shall only emphasize here that such skill is of the utmost importance in transformational psychotherapy.

Having acquired the skills of being able to be involved, yet also stand apart, and to perform executive functions in therapy, the therapist's consciousness is then available for observation of behavior within and without. In this work there is greater emphasis on observation of the client's external behavior, with the flexibility, of course, to observe anything relevant within or without. What to observe, and in what frame of reference, is discussed in later chapters.

## *Goal Orientation*

Another piece of the training of most psychotherapists that is relevant in transformational psychotherapy is the ability to formulate goals and to recognize when they have been achieved.

Not every psychotherapy clearly delineates goals for therapy. Some forms of psychotherapy may be designed simply for the personal education of the individual. An example of this might be a training psychoanalysis. Many people in a training psychoanalysis do not call this a form of psychotherapy and simply support the idea that this is personal education.

When a psychoanalyst is employed for therapy purposes, he or she must be cognizant of the goals of treatment. Any truly good psychotherapy training program teaches the formulation of goals in therapy and how to recognize them as having been achieved.

In this regard it is better to have positively formulated goals than negatively formulated goals. For example, it would be better to formulate a goal of treatment as "the development of autonomy" in certain areas, rather than the "eradication" of a certain symptom. This is not to say that the eradication of symptomatology is a disservice to anyone, but once the symptom has been eradicated, what do we then observe? Those training programs that emphasize the issues of health rather than the eradication of illness make positive goal formulation the focal point of the practitioner.

For the purposes of transformational therapy it is helpful to formulate goals clearly and to know about them consciously. Thus the duration of treatment will be related to achieving goals rather than to the amount of time spent in the process. This attitude supports the formulation of appropriate strategies, as opposed to mere adherence to ritualistic behavior by the therapist and client. The goal oriented therapist may have a variety of methods to reach the goal, with none considered more precious than another. Methodology becomes interchangeable. Creativity and responsible experimentation are encouraged. There is an air of excitement and discovery in the psychotherapeutic process itself.

Unfortunately, if the therapist becomes method oriented rather than goal oriented, the process sometimes overstays its welcome, and goals may be forgotten after a while. Both therapist and client may feel they are "putting in time" and hope to achieve goals by good attendance records. No one ever wants this to occur, but it is a common clinical experience of many psychotherapists who have overinvested in a single method of treatment.

## CLINICAL RESPONSIBILITY

What is the extent of the therapist's responsibility? What do we mean by responsibility in this frame of reference, and what are its limits?

Common use of the term "responsibility" in the sense of accountability usually focuses on the outcome of an action rather than what precedes it. In other words, responsibility usually is considered the accountability for blame or credit. Blame and credit are considerations after an event has occurred.

Our emphasis here, however, is on the other side of responsibility, namely, accountability *before* the event has occurred. The event that is being judged came *from* the person or thing held accountable. The source precedes the event. Blame or credit follows the event. When we deal with transformational processes, we are interested in leverage, in a factor increase in the realm of power in a process. Therefore in this work we concentrate on that which produces an event—the key operational locus.

Within this frame of reference the therapist is "responsible" for the psychotherapy, for the context of personal transformation. The client is "responsible" for making the transformation occur.

Although it can be said that personal transformation can occur in an instant of psychological time, the *manifestation* of change and the full integration, understanding, and acceptance of it by the client occurs over days, weeks, or months of physical time. When a therapist accepts a client in a transformational process, the clinical responsibility parallels that of mainstream psychotherapy in that the therapist agrees to provide a context for appropriate and complete change through time, and, in addition, provides not only the context of transformation, but also the context of the unfolding of the transformation.

Responsibility can be delegated. Standard business management dictates that when responsibility is delegated, appropriate authority should accompany it. In other words, one should have the power to carry out one's delegated duties. At the point when the client is ready to participate in continued transformation through life beyond an ongoing relationship with a psychotherapist, the formal relationship can be terminated. In effect, responsibility for the context for change has been delegated to the client, who, by means of the experience through time of developing abilities, is empowered to carry out the task. Thus at the end of a full and complete psychotherapy, both responsibilities are held by the client: the responsibility to produce the change and the responsibility to create a continued context for such development.

Training in clinical responsibility is available in any good psychotherapy training program. It is a skill, which involves clarifying the fine line between therapist and client resources. If therapist and client were each static entities, this would be an easy skill to acquire. By locating the line between the two sets of resources, one can find out where the responsibilities lie. However, these entities are not static, but are changing and evolving. Therefore, clinical responsibility is constantly under examination and negotiation, with respect to extent.

In addition to medical and psychotherapy training programs, there is one other area where clinical responsibility can be taught that is rarely regarded in such a manner, that is, the area of parenting. The roles of the parent for the newborn, for three-month-, six-month-, one-year-, two-year-, and three-year-old children, and so on, are very different. These roles do not change suddenly. Day by day parents should recognize how much children can do by themselves, and how much parental guidance is necessary.

CHAPTER

# 2

# RAPPORT

Webster defines "rapport" as

> relation of harmony, conformity, accord, or affinity, especially as *in rapport*—in an intimate or harmonious relation.[1]

Rapport is one of the vital ingredients in a transformational psychotherapy. In fact, to be in harmony with another human being can even be a goal in one's own personal life; it can truly be a goal in itself. In this work, however, it is an ingredient in the process. Because rapport is so special, in fact, precious, it is quite understandable that there would be the following two schools of thought about rapport.

One school of thought takes the position that rapport cannot be learned; it is inherent in human interaction. The other school takes the position that it can be taught and learned. In certain ways they are both correct. The capacity for rapport is inherent in the human nervous system. In the given individual it may be less or more developed. Just as with any other capacity, if one has not yet fully developed one's capacity for rapport, one can learn to uncover, refine, and develop it. This process is the study of rapport skills training.

Rapport is a key ingredient in transformational psychotherapy, since the relationship between client and therapist in a transformational process is

[1]*Webster's New Collegiate Dictionary*, 6th ed., s.v. "rapport."

very special. It is true that the relationship between client and therapist is always special in any therapy process. But in a transformational psychotherapy there are other dimensions.

For example, whereas in most mainstream psychotherapies symbiosis between client and therapist would be considered undesirable and pathological, there are moments in transformational work where it simply cannot proceed without such intimate biofeedback loops. To discern between pathological symbiosis and the creative intimacy of hypnotic communication is basic to the understanding of the ingredient of rapport. Hypnotic communication keeps directorial functioning of the "ego," or the mind of the therapist, outside the manifest operation itself, enabling the external process to proceed with as pure a flow of mutual feedback as possible.

The untrained observer seeing only the interaction would consider it symbiotic. The trained observer knows that what is *not* seen is the direction and purpose of the operator, guiding the interaction very explicitly along certain strategic guidelines.

When people are in perfect rapport they frequently transcend reaction time. An extreme example of reaction time would be found in a chess game. Player A makes a move. In response, several minutes later, Player B makes a move. In response to that move, several minutes later, Player A makes a move.

An example of transcendence of reaction time would be a large choir singing well together. If each singer had to wait even a small fraction of a second for the other to begin it would sound absolutely chaotic. The fractions would add up, and people would be totally out of synchrony. Instead, each individual responds to the main, or central, structure and rhythm, and the result is unity among all.

Rapport and absence of reaction time are not causally related. They are simply found together frequently. In other words, when a point of maximum rapport is achieved there is usually a shift from "reacting to" another to "reacting with" another. For a more detailed discussion of this subject see the section on "Pacing and Leading" in Chapter 3.

## RAPPORT TRAINING

In the first section of this chapter we discussed the two major schools of thought with respect to the concept of rapport. The first school claims that rapport cannot be learned; one either can get in rapport with others, or one cannot. The second school claims that rapport can be learned. For our purposes a discussion of the second school is more profitable.

The school that says one can be trained to establish rapport essentially has methods that involve reaction time as intrinsic to the *training*. However, after the training period, one is instructed to drop the training, let integration occur, and essentially leave it to the unconscious mind to monitor. Ultimately this enables reaction time to drop out and rapport to emerge. Both schools require spontaneity as an ingredient; but the second school brings skill and learning into spontaneity. As long as the reader keeps in mind that the following are training strategies, ultimately to be dropped in their training form, and in practice to be integrated into the personality of the therapist, to be used spontaneously, then all this will make sense. Misapplication of the method, that is, using the training method in a clinical situation directly, could, at the very least, seem rather strange to the client and would most probably interfere with or entirely destroy rapport.

The basic principle is *to meet the client in the client's model of the world*. Much will be developed on this theme throughout this book.

As we move further into the subject we begin to discover that the most powerful rapport training strategies involve emphasis on *form* rather than *content*. Here "content" refers to the subject matter in the communication. "Form," on the other hand, involves *how* the communication itself is proceeding. For example, no matter what the subject matter is, if one party is speaking in French and the other is speaking in Japanese, rapport might be very difficult to achieve. If both parties switched to gesture and pantomime in order to communicate their intentions, rapport might increase.

## Rapport Strategies of Form

### *Kinesics*

This is a well-studied subject frequently referred to as "body language." A great deal can be found on this subject in the communications literature, and for our purposes an example or two might suffice. A good analogue would be dance rather than conversation.

If the interaction between therapist and client is thought of *as if* it were a dance, then attention to rhythm and position would make sense. A rather remarkable example of the use of kinesics is known as "mirroring." Simply using the same tilt of the head, breathing rate, or general posture of the other, can lead more rapidly to mutuality than actual agreement on the issues of content.

Mirroring, however, has pitfalls just as great as the rewards. If mirroring is done with noticeable reaction time, or is overdone to the point of caricature—perceived as such by the other person—it can easily destroy rapport. The other person will think that you are either making fun of or bizarrely copying his or her movements. When reaction time drops as close to zero as possible, as it does in a well-performed dance when it is hard to know who is initiating the movement (if even "initiation of movement" is an appropriate concept), there is a profound experience of affinity.

What enables people to drop reaction time in a well-performed dance is that they are each relating to a factor *outside* the dyad, i.e., the music. The external rhythms become internalized and self-generating. If the music stops abruptly one can keep dancing. As "music" is to "dancing," the "model of the world" is to "rapport."

### *Representational Systems*

It is well known that the human brain is receiving and processing an astronomical amount of input, at any given time, from the external world as well as the internal environment. It is also a well-known fact that the human brain organizes much of its information according to its sensory systems, which can be divided, for simplicity, into the visual, auditory, olfactory and gustatory, and kinesthetic systems. Here the term "kinesthetic" refers to tactile and proprioceptive sensory data and to the emotions, which from a purely mechanistic or neurologic position could be understood as mechanical/physical responses. Although there are other ways to organize our thinking about the sensory systems, it is useful for us to consider these four realms—visual, auditory, olfactory/gustatory, and kinesthetic—as the four basic realms, in view of the current highly valuable neurolinguistic programming literature in which this four-map system is used.[2]

Although these sensory systems interrelate, they also have vast networks

---

[2]John Grinder and R. Bandler, *The Structure of Magic*, vol. 2 (Palo Alto, CA: Science and Behavior Books, Inc., 1976), pt 1, pp. 1–26.

that appear to be autonomous. A particular sound (auditory system) might relate experientially to a certain color (visual system), but on the whole the visual and auditory systems are autonomous, producing color and sound, independently.

For our purposes, in the study of rapport, it is worthwhile to realize that we organize our experience of the world within these systems. The considerations of *content* might be quite independent of the sensory map(s) in which we process the information.

For example, "to understand" could be processed according to different senses. Visually, to "understand" would mean to "*see* it all clearly" and have "*perspective*." Kinesthetically, to "understand" would mean to have a "grasp" or "handle" on it all. Auditorially, to "understand" would be to "tune in" on it, so that it really "sounds" right. And so on.

Consistent with the rapport principle of meeting the client in the client's model of the world, one way to maximize rapport would be to ascertain what sensory system or systems the client is using at the given moment and to participate in those systems.[3]

The following two examples illustrate the above:

1. *Maximizing Rapport*

CLIENT: Things appear to be rather gloomy and dark these days. [*Visual* Map: "appear," "dark," etc.]

THERAPIST: Perhaps you can give me more of a picture as to what's going on. Let's try to focus in more. [*Visual* Map: "picture," "focus"]

CLIENT: Fine. I'd like to.

2. *Minimizing Rapport*

CLIENT: Things appear to be rather gloomy and dark these days. [*Visual*]

THERAPIST: Sounds like you feel bad. Right? [*Auditory*: "sounds"; *Kinesthetic*: "feel"]

CLIENT: What?

It is impressive how the most well-meaning therapist desiring to sympathize with the client's deep upset might actually destroy rapport, as in the second example, by a clash of *form* rather than of *content*. By simply communicating in a different sensory system than the one in which the

---

[3]Ibid.

client is representing his or her world, the therapist has not met the client in the client's model of the world and is essentially out of harmony.

In the first example, however, the therapist did meet the client in the same sensory system, visual, and so the communication could proceed with greater rapport. In the study of representational systems, it becomes, then, a significant matter to be able to ascertain what system the client is in at any given moment. This study involves some of the basic building blocks in the field of neurolinguistic programming.[4] Once the therapist is aware that every individual is constantly offering information as to which sensory map is being used, an entire new realm for exploration and understanding is opened.

## Accessing Cues

People are constantly giving clues as to what sensory map they are using for processing data. In the neurolinguistic programming literature these clues are known as "cues," particularly "accessing cues."[5]

Naturally the therapist must use his or her own senses in order to discover what the client is doing. The following sections are organized under the therapist's own sensory channels, that is to say, what can be detected by the therapist's hearing, seeing, and kinesthetic sensing.

### *Auditory Sense of the Therapist*

**Predicates.** Paying attention (listening) to language and linguistics while in the presence of the client, particularly to the use of verbs and adjectives, that is to say, the descriptive words, is one of the easiest methods for the beginner. As in the examples given above, the use of verbs and adjectives that were specifically related to certain sensory systems of the client were at the heart of the matter. As will be outlined below, the client's use of language is not the *only* way in which one can know how the client is processing information.

---

[4]R. Dilts, J. Grinder, R. Bandler, L. C. Bandler, and J. DeLozier, *Neuro-Linguistic Programming*, vol. 1 (Cupertino, CA: Meta Publications, 1980), p. 17.

[5]John Grinder, J. DeLozier, and R. Bandler, *Patterns of the Hypnotic Techniques of Milton H. Erickson, M.D.*, vol. 2 (Cupertino, CA: Meta Publications, 1977), pp. 34–37 (hereafter cited as *Erickson Hypnotic Techniques*, vol. 2).

The technique of *matching* predicates,[6] that is, responding in the same system verbally that the client is operating in, is a skill that can be learned and ultimately integrated and utilized. An important principle is as follows: When experiencing rapport with a client, continue in that manner. However, when not in rapport with a client, briefly shift awareness from the content issues to the representational systems that the client is using and *meet the client in that system*, perhaps by matching predicates. This usually results in a powerful positive shift in the atmosphere in which the communication is taking place.

**Tonality.** Obviously it would be useful to have a *variety* of ways to detect the given representational system, in addition to listening to predicates. One other area of the therapist's ability to listen is in the *tonality* of the voice of the client. Interestingly enough, in many people, there is an association of high, middle, and lower tones with visual, auditory, and kinesthetic mapping, in that order. In other words, an individual speaking in the higher registers of voice is often using his visual mapping system; lower register, kinesthetic system, and so on. "Calibration" enters as a useful concept at this point.

## *Calibration*

Calibration is a term used in the neurolinguistic literature to describe the process of perceiving each individual as a unique case. For example, although everybody has fingerprints, each fingerprint is different. It is possible that when most people are using their lower voice registers, they are also mapping in a kinesthetic area, and when they are using their higher tones, they are in a visual map. However, this may not be the case universally. Therefore, it is important to find out by skillful interviewing, observation, and listening the correlation of voice tone with sensory map for each unique individual.

It is obvious that calibration can require much practice and attentiveness. It is also important to note that this is, without doubt, a learnable skill.

The principle underlying calibration is simply that generalizations are

[6]Grinder and Bandler, *Structure of Magic*, pp. 16–19.

generalizations, but people are unique. One does not attempt to make people conform to the generalizations.

The cues presented here, then, are guidelines that serve to orient to the manner in which most people appear and sound when they are accessing (utilizing) certain sensory systems.[7]

## *Visual Sense of the Therapist*

Theoretically, if one simply used tonality of voice and matching of predicates, rapport could be achieved in a purely auditory communication system, such as a telephone conversation or two-way radio, or in those therapy situations where face-to-face contact is minimized, such as psychoanalysis.

**General observation.** It is also possible by simply *watching* and observing certain of the client's kinesics that one may also detect what sensory system the client is using. With respect to what to watch specifically, one advanced technique involves observing *any* available kinesic whatsoever. For example, it is possible that every time a particular individual is in his visual map he twitches his left wrist in a peculiar manner; when he is processing information in an auditory map, his eyebrows are raised; and when he is on a kinesthetic map his right wrist moves. These examples are highly specific to one hypothetical individual; therefore, such idiosyncratic cues really require a trained eye to detect.

**Eye-accessing cues.** One of the easiest ways to develop such a trained eye would be to deal with certain accessing cues that are universal, or close to universal, rather than "any" observable phenomena specific to a given individual. For example, there are certain eye movements that are known in the neurolinguistic programming literature as the *eye-accessing cues.*[8] These tend to be common to most people in this culture.

Before going any further, one might wonder why bother doing this, if simply listening to predicates would be sufficient. The fact is that simply listening to predicates is not sufficient. Occasionally a client will use

---

[7]Dilts et al., *Neuro-Linguistic Programming*, p. 17.

[8]Grinder, DeLozier, and Bandler, *Erickson Hypnotic Techniques*, vol. 2, p. 35.

*nonspecific* predicates, yet will actually be operating within a highly specific sensory realm. In other words, a person might say, "*I understand*," while in the process of internal visualization—using images. "Understand" is not specific to any given sensory modality. The person is not saying "I have the *picture*" or "I *see* it all clearly"—visual predicates. The client is simply saying "I understand."

However, if tonality of the voice was monitored, and it was observed that a low tonality was associated with kinesthetic mapping and a high tonality with visual mapping, then the therapist is ready for the following. When the person says "I understand" with a *low* tone of voice (kinesthetic), and at a later point says "I understand" with a *high* tone of voice (visual), it is appreciated that these are two different types of "understanding" located in two different realms of the nervous system. This allows the therapist, for the purpose of rapport, to respond with predicates to match those areas. The client has been met in the client's model of the world even though *words* did not reveal what sensory map was being used.

With respect to the eye movements, they basically divide into three areas: (1) *upward* scanning left and right, (2) *horizontal* scanning left and right, and (3) *downward* scanning left and right. Left and right refer here to the client's left and right.

A great deal has been written about this subject in the work of Richard Bandler and John Grinder, *The Structure of Magic*, Vols. I and II, as well as other publications in the neurolinguistic programming literature. It would be redundant to go into as thorough a description as they give in their work.

For our purposes it will be sufficient simply to say the following. These three areas of eye movements indicate sensory maps that the client is operating within at the time the eyes are in that area. The following table will show the areas.[9]

| Eye Movements | Sensory Map |
|---|---|
| Up | Visual |
| Horizontal | Auditory |
| Down Left | Auditory |
| Down Right | Kinesthetic |

[9]Ibid.

The subject of this chapter is rapport, not neurolinguistic programming. In the field of neurolinguistic programming, finer distinctions are made regarding subdivisions of eye movement patterns. For our purposes the above is sufficient.

To simplify matters even more, the above information can be used in the following manner. If you ask someone, "Do you understand?" and the person looks *up* and then back at you saying, "Yes," it is likely that they have made an internal image and visualized in order to "understand."

If you ask someone "Do you understand?" and they look *down to their right*, and look back at you saying "Yes," it is likely that they have used a kinesthetic map to "understand."

This becomes more interesting when the eyes rapidly shift in many directions. One discovers that, in fact, there are specific rapid sequences that the person might go through from one sensory area to another, and then to another, possibly even recycling inefficiently, in order to process information and handle the mental task. All of this information is useful in neurolinguistic programming[10] and to some degree in the study of rapport.

As stated before, each realm of study indicated in this book is truly endless. This is not to be discouraging but, on the contrary, to remind the reader that mastery can be increased in any field endlessly. It is not necessary to know what all the eye movements mean. However, it is necessary to know that eye movements mean something.

One example of a slightly more complex pattern might be when the client is asked, "Do you understand?" and the client looks (1) up, then (2) down right, then (3) down left, then (4) back to down right again, and then says "Yes." In sensory terms, the sequence was (1) visual, (2) kinesthetic, (3) auditory, and (4) kinesthetic.

Actually this opens an option for the therapist to respond by *sequencing* predicates to the client in the same sensory terms. This can lead to profound rapport. For example, "It seems that you *pictured* it, got some *sense* of it, *told* yourself something about it, which *felt* right about it." This statement is meaningful to the client, although on examination of the content rather than the form, it is absolutely meaningless. However, it is the form that is meaningful to the client. The meaning communicated is that the ther-

---

[10]Dilts et al., *Neuro-Linguistic Programming*, pp. 26–59.

apist is meeting the client in the client's model of the world, whether or not there is agreement. The message is "I am here with you."

**Superficial skin vessels and facial muscle tension.** When one moves into even finer tuning of the visual sense, one can begin to notice that it is possible that a person might blush or have a redder skin tone while in one sensory map, and lighter tone when in another. It is possible that a person might furrow the brow or have tighter skin muscles visible to the eye due to increased creases in the skin during one sensory modality of thinking than in another.

It is useful to know that this occurs, whether or not one can immediately apply this information. There are no studies to date as to what is common throughout the culture. Even if there were, ultimately it is a matter of calibration to the given client.

## *Tactile Sense of the Therapist*

There are very few psychotherapies in which it is appropriate in our culture for the therapist to touch the client for any length of time. The spectrum ranges all the way from psychoanalysis, in which there is not only minimal touching but minimal visual contact of client to therapist, all the way to the systems of therapy and personal encounter where a hand on the client is appropriate.

The purpose of this section is not to recommend touching, but to bring to your awareness that one can ascertain what sensory system a person is thinking in by merely touching the person. At first this might sound uncanny. The facts are that this does not refer to "touching" in the layman's sense. Any skilled physician has learned that the tactile sense can give a great deal of information as to the condition of the patient. This finding is in the best medical diagnostic tradition.

If there is any fundamental rule of rapport it might be: Be appropriate. Be appropriate to your client's sensory systems. Be appropriate to the culture. Be appropriate to all forces and constraints in the system.

Even though one might be able to ascertain by touch what sensory system an individual is processing in, if the person is in a psychotherapy in which touching has never been done, then some other way must be used to detect the person's system. However, if touching is appropriate in the given situation, the following data are useful: *temperature* and *skin moisture*.

In some training seminars students are divided into groups of five persons each. One person plays "the subject," another plays the "interviewer." The remaining three are arranged in the following positions: one places a hand gently on the back of the subject's neck; another stands near the subject facing away, just listening; and the third, to which we will pay attention, has both hands on the subject's left hand.

The job of the "interviewer" is simply to conduct an interview in which the subject needs to move attention into various sensory areas, visual, auditory, and kinesthetic. While that is occurring, the person touching the back of the neck detects subtle changes in temperature of the skin on the back of the neck, corresponding to the given sensory modality—visual, auditory, or kinesthetic.

The person standing nearby listening to the voice of the subject is to detect changes only in tonality, not predicates.

The person touching the left hand is to detect on the surface of the hand any changes in skin moisture and temperature. The results of such an experiment vary from subject to subject. The following findings are from one actual trial, and are offered as an example.

When the subject was experiencing pictures, the hand was dry and of moderate temperature. The moment the person began discussing feelings of any kind (kinesthetic) the palm was warmer and fingers and palm became slightly moist. In some cases it may take several attempts to notice finer distinctions. Yet with a given individual it may be possible to know, *by touch*, and particularly the feel of the palmar aspect of the hand, in what sensory modality they are experiencing the world at any given time.

In no way does this information by itself reveal its relevance to the therapist. The value is simply in knowing that this can occur.

If we know that by listening to a client, by looking at a client, and by touching (when appropriate) a client, and calibrating the received information to the specific client's experience, we can quite accurately determine what mode of sensory experience the client is having at that point in time, then we have more tools to meet the client in the client's model of the world—direct tools of rapport. When these tools are integrated into our own system they become skills.

Just like learning to drive a car, ride a bicycle, or operate any machine, at first the complexity of the task can be overwhelming. Later on we learn to integrate the material into our personality. Similarly, when we have integrated this material into our interviewing skills, we no longer pay much attention consciously to the experience. It is all handled unconsciously by the nervous system's ability to master complex information. The resulting experience can be simply that of getting along a lot better with clients, and experiencing more rapport with others without knowing consciously what it is that is working so well.[11]

## EMPATHY

The dictionary defines empathy as "*imaginative projection of one's own consciousness into another being.*"[12] When dealing with the subject of rapport as a practical clinical consideration, it is important that "imaginative projection" be accurate.

Empathy can also be trained. Such training can ensure that imaginative projection be based on processes in which the probability is higher that the imaginings of the therapist are close to the experience of the client.

The use of empathy to achieve rapport has its risks. If the therapist is dealing with a client who is depressed, and wants to find out what it is like in order to be with that client, he or she might have to get depressed temporarily. If a client is going through tension accompanied by abdominal difficulties, the therapist may have to experience similar abdominal symptoms in order to work with the client.

Nevertheless, empathy remains a very powerful means of establishing rapport, and can be used safely and in a highly rewarding manner in those areas where experiencing the client's world directly is fundamentally safe with respect to the therapist's well-being.

Some of the best training for empathy has its roots in psychodrama and the theoretical work of J. L. Moreno, M.D.[13] The two principle techniques in psychodrama that can train or expand one's capacity for empathy are *reversing roles* and *doubling*. A brief description follows to clarify the meaning of these terms and to impart a sense of how one can achieve an

---

[11]In order to get started in practicing some of the skills utilizing representational systems, a sample format can be found in Grinder, DeLozier, and Bandler, *Erickson Hypnotic Techniques*, vol. 2, p. 36. For an experiential approach to neurolinguistic programming, the reader may obtain information regarding workshops throughout the country from Not Ltd., Division of Training and Research, 517 Mission Street, Santa Cruz, CA 95060.

[12]*Webster's New Collegiate Dictionary*, 6th ed., s.v. "empathy."

[13]J.L. Moreno, *Who Shall Survive?* (Beacon, NY: Beacon House, Inc., 1953).

expanded capacity for empathy by using them. (Further discussion of psychodrama is in Chapter 6.)

## Role Reversal

Role reversal is simply a technique in which a person physically exchanges roles with another person in the drama (situation). For example, imagine a play in which an actor is in a scene playing the "father" and another actor is playing the "son." If the actor playing "father" were rehearsing on a day that the actor playing "son" was absent, the same actor could play the "father" role and then move to the other part of the stage where the "son" would be and read the "son's" line in the same way that the absent actor would have read it. In fact, at that moment, an understudy could stand in for "father." Thus the single actor could move back and forth between the two roles.

Similarly, in therapy if the therapist wanted to understand a dynamic of a particular client, it could be done in the client's absence, using role reversal. In the privacy of the office one could do the following experiential exercise. Facing the client's empty chair and sitting in the therapist's chair, the therapist imagines the client in the empty chair. The therapist begins an imagined interview.

The therapist then gets out of the chair, sits in the chair of the client, assumes the posture of the client, and gets into "first-person" sort of thinking about the client, such as, "My name is *(client's name)*. I live at *(client's address)*; and my brothers and sisters are *(client's siblings)*; and these days my life has been as follows *(delivers a monologue of what that is like)*." From this position a great deal will be learned by the therapist. The therapist is no longer being "the therapist." The therapist is now actually portraying the client. In fact the therapist, from the new position, gains insight as to the ways in which the client perceives the therapist across the room.

The extent that the character or "role" of the client is fully developed in its parameters by the person portraying the client will be the extent that this will be effective as a tool of empathy. Caricature of the client will fail to produce the desired result, but true role reversal will produce the desired result. Obviously this is a high-voltage technique if the client's condition is in any way disturbed to a serious degree.

The antidote for having developed any of the client's characteristics while in the chair is to simply get out of the chair and return to the therapist's position, leaving the "imaginary" client in the empty chair and regaining the role of therapist in the psychodrama.

The mechanism for the strength of this technique is discussed in Chapter 3, particularly the section on "anchoring." After actually using this technique a number of times it can be available to the therapist purely mentally, without having to get out of the chair.

## Doubling

The technique of *doubling* is another technique used in psychodrama to amplify and further elucidate the client's inner thoughts and feelings. In psychodrama the client (known as the *protagonist*) might be addressing another individual on the psychodrama stage. The double is another member of the group, possibly a cotherapist, who stands *next* to the protagonist in approximately the same body posture and says those things that the double thinks are true but unsaid by the protagonist, in order to amplify and get closer to the inner feelings and thoughts.

For example, the scene is the protagonist with a sibling. Double standing next to the protagonist. Group member standing in for the sibling.

PROTAGONIST [*to the sibling*]: I don't like you!

DOUBLE [*loud voice*]: I can't stand you!!!

This leaves the protagonist the option to accept or reject that statement. The protagonist might say:

PROTAGONIST: No. No. That isn't true. I just don't like you.

Or the protagonist might shout:

PROTAGONIST: Yes! That's true! I do hate you!

DOUBLE: . . . and I also love you.

which may lead the protagonist to consider positive feelings at that point, or to continue in the catharsis.

In order for the person playing the double to say the "right things" at the time, and not to have his or her communications constantly being rejected by the protagonist, the double needs to empathize fully with the protagonist. The goal in psychodrama is not empathy training. The goal is to assist the protagonist via doubling to amplify and fully explore his or her feelings, and ultimately to resolve them. The by-product, or the means, of doubling is empathy.

One way that a person might develop rapport skills by means of empathy would be to participate in psychodrama training groups available in many of the major cities throughout the country, paying particular attention to the techniques of role reversal and doubling as sources of learning. Of course, it is possible, as mentioned above, to adapt these particular methods usually found in psychodrama groups to the private practitioner's office, where appropriate. Interestingly enough, when adapted to the private office, the methods might not even require the presence of the client in order to establish a degree of empathy, but purely by enhancing the imaginative projection of the therapist.

Therefore we can understand that rapport is far from being a matter of innate talent. Of course, there are some people who intuitively have developed skills in this area so that by the time they become professional therapists they are able to achieve rapport with most people under most circumstances. To some degree we all have been able to develop skills of rapport. What has been emphasized in this chapter is that therapists can actually expand their ability to achieve rapport with clients, and in transformational psychotherapy the ability to achieve rapport is a vital and necessary component to the process. It is the communicational link or bond between the individuals in the transaction, without which the transaction could not occur.

The next chapter will deal with hypnosis and hypnotic communication. Many of the issues discussed in this first section, relating to preparatory skills, overlap and intersect. It is difficult to achieve effective hypnotic communication without rapport. One might even wonder if in a true state of rapport there is not hypnotic communication.

As mentioned earlier, these preparatory skill chapters are to be read first, so that all of the chapters can begin to integrate at once. The reader will notice a linearity or a sequential presentation occurring from chapter to chapter and from point to point within each chapter. This is only an artifact of language. All of these issues interrelate and are simply being focused on one at a time.

CHAPTER

# 3

# HYPNOSIS AND HYPNOTIC COMMUNICATION

## HYPNOSIS

Hypnosis and rapport are different issues entirely, yet they seem to be woven from the same fabric and are so closely interrelated that it is almost impossible to discuss the one without somehow discussing the other. The more one learns about the field of hypnosis and the capacity of human beings to utilize altered states of consciousness to produce results, the more amazing it becomes that this subject is not a *requirement* of the training of the professional psychotherapist.

Hypnosis is an area that deals directly with portions of the human psyche that are only touched upon indirectly with other methods. This is not to say that indirect methods are inappropriate. In fact, at times indirect approaches are the most effective. Yet, never to be exposed to direct interaction with the unconscious mind in one's basic training is indeed unfortunate. Working directly with the human unconscious is so impressive that it has inspired the greatest thinkers in psychology of our time, among them Sigmund Freud.

The unconscious mind is not only the seat of primitive wishes, fantasies, incestuous drives, cannibalistic thoughts, and the collective demonic jungle of our planet. Also in residence there we can discover the capacity for ingenious problem solving, nonlinear solutions, the ability to create pictures worth a thousand words, and curative and healing metaphor; indeed the unconscious contains the very wellspring of evolution and transformation.

To the uninitiated the subject of hypnosis brings to mind coercion, manipulation, and theatrics of the worst kind. To the sophisticated practitioner with the deepest regard for what is precious in the human being, the study of hypnosis can become a gateway to our untapped multidimensional qualities. From a practical standpoint this would imply that hypnosis is an endless study. That is absolutely correct.

Almost anything worth holding our interest might also have that quality. Pragmatically speaking, we will be bringing our attention to the minimum rather than the maximum to be explored and mastered in order to accomplish transformational therapy. We will then be able to say that less than that amount is not sufficient for the job, and beyond that is for your interest, study, and further mastery. With this in mind, it makes sense then that this subject can be addressed in a single chapter in a book. There are volumes—even whole libraries—on the subject of hypnosis. This chapter will delineate only what practitioners need to know minimally to get the job done.

Much has been said so far regarding transformation occurring in an instant of psychological time. During that instant there is a shift in the set in which circumstances or specifics are being held. (More of this will be discussed in Chapter 5.) Using the techniques of mainstream psychotherapies, a set may also change even with relatively indirect methods. The purpose of hypnosis and hypnotic communication in transformational psychotherapy is that it provides the technology, the wherewithal deep enough to deal *directly* with the shifting of a set or a context. Just as in dreams it is possible to instantaneously create changes that would be considered impossible or outlandish in the waking state, so it is easy to make large moves in a hypnotic trance that would be extremely difficult to do in the waking state. Great sweeps of creativity can enter internal psychological worlds. Shifts can occur with a few words. Perception itself becomes the playing field. Proper application of hypnotic techniques in psychotherapy would be like the application of architecture to the structure of human experience.

Before going further, there are certain ethical considerations. The ethical standards outlined by the American Society of Clinical Hypnosis and/or the Society for Clinical and Experimental Hypnosis are perfectly adequate.

The reader is referred to these societies directly for details.[1] Principally, their standards state that practitioners should have proven in their respective fields that they are capable of being trusted in such a delicate situation.

It is true that there are many excellent healers in other cultures who use hypnosis at least as responsibly (and at times even more effectively) as many practitioners of hypnosis in our culture. Therefore, the issue is not academic study, but competency linked with clinical responsibility. Essentially, what it takes to be ethical in the fields of psychotherapy, medicine, and dentistry is what it takes to be ethical in the use of hypnosis.

## Minimum Standards of Competency

Technically, all that is necessary in order to use hypnosis in transformational psychotherapy is to be able to (1) induce a hypnotic trance, (2) utilize it for treatment goals, and (3) bring the client out of trance fully. Realizing that these three items constitute no more and no less than a minimum level, newcomers to the field can know with certainty that when they can perform these three functions with a sense of ease and competency, they have achieved the necessary minimum level. As a rule, these skills are easily and rapidly acquired during introductory training courses in hypnosis, particularly those sponsored by the societies mentioned in the last section. That is to say, on the basic level the material is not especially difficult; one needs only a desire to learn it.

The reader is warned that fascination increases exponentially when moving from the basic level to the intermediate level of study.

## Definitions of Hypnosis

There are many good definitions of hypnosis throughout the literature. They vary from author to author, from the highly behavioral and operational kinds of language to the more mystical and religious. This can be somewhat bewildering to the newcomer in the field. The following remarks might be useful in understanding the variety of definitions.

It is always easier to understand a concept from the point of view of the

[1]The American Society of Clinical Hypnosis, 2400 East Devon Avenue, Suite 218, Des Plaines, IL 60018; The Society for Clinical and Experimental Hypnosis, 129-A Kings Park Drive, Liverpool, NY 13088.

larger set that encloses it. The larger set in which hypnosis is included is the field of altered states of consciousness. Preferably the term should be "alternative" states of consciousness, but this expression rarely occurs in the literature.

The human being is capable of going through many different states of consciousness in any given 24-hour period.[2] This is the way we live our lives, and the experience is so familiar to us that we might not notice it in the same way that a fish might not notice the water in which it is swimming. The state of consciousness you are in when the alarm rings in the morning is not the same state of consciousness you were in in the dream that just preceded the alarm clock ringing. The state of consciousness you are in while performing ablutions might not be the same state of consciousness you are in while traveling to work. Although some states of consciousness have been formally named (e.g., fugue states, hypnogogic states, dreams, meditative states, drug-induced states, intense concentration), it would be much easier to simply realize that a human being normally experiences a constant fluctuation in state of consciousness throughout the day. Many of the fluctuations might not even be noticed, while many others are perceived.

For example, the state of consciousness one is in when learning to drive a car is not the same state one is in when normally driving a car. Learning to drive a car involves a great deal of concentration on every move, whereas normal driving occurs with a great deal of automaticity, so much so that the driver can even have a conversation with another person while driving.

When it comes to a working definition of hypnosis, it is far more useful to restrict that term to a description of the following kind of event: hypnosis is an altered state of consciousness in which a person is highly responsive to cues and signals from the hypnotist on a level of automaticity.

A universal definition is desirable. In the field of hypnosis, it is a bit late. The term hypnosis is used in so many different ways. There are those in the literature who prefer to call any altered state of consciousness "hypnosis," leading to questions such as, "Isn't meditation really hypnosis?" "Isn't advertising or an effective political speech really hypnosis?" If one uses the term "hypnosis" for every altered state of consciousness, then

---

[2]Charles C. Tart, ed., *Altered States of Consciousness* (Garden City, NY: Anchor Books, Doubleday and Co., Inc., 1969).

anything is really hypnosis. If we restrict the term to the kind of event described by the working definition above, then we can be more precise.[3]

My own personal and professional preference in this area is to consider hypnosis to be communication with the unconscious mind with the goal of eliciting responses from the unconscious without the need of involvement of the conscious mind in order to affect such responses. This would be more of a communications model of hypnosis and has application in the work of transformational psychotherapy.

With hypnosis held as an effective and productive communication skill, the entire field becomes an integral part of the psychotherapeutic arena.

## Hypnosis and Representational Systems

In the previous chapter we brought our attention to representational systems: visual, auditory, kinesthetic, and olfactory/gustatory. The emphasis was on these neural mechanisms as the means of interpreting internal and external data flowing through the nervous system. From this point of view a technology of rapport becomes quite understandable. In this chapter we will build another dimension to the utilization of representational systems by realizing that altered states of consciousness also take place within these systems.

It appears clinically that people tend to favor one representational system over another, particularly in relation to the given state of consciousness.[4] While driving a car, for example, a person may primarily emphasize the visual system, whereas during lovemaking the kinesthetic system may be emphasized. These considerations become especially relevant in therapeutic applications. The given representational system predominating during what would be called the "conscious" or "waking" state may be thought of as a map that is complete in many ways with little room for unexplored

---

[3]For further understanding of the dilemma of defining hypnosis, the reader is referred to Martin T. Orne, "On the Construct of Hypnosis: How Its Definition Affects Research and Its Clinical Application," in *Handbook of Hypnosis and Psychosomatic Medicine*, ed. Graham D. Burrows and Lorraine Dennerstein (New York: Elsevier North-Holland, 1980), chap. 3, pp. 29–51.

[4]John Grinder, J. DeLozier, and R. Bandler, *Patterns of the Hypnotic Techniques of Milton H. Erickson, M.D.*, vol. 2 (Cupertino, CA: Meta Publications, 1977) (hereafter cited as *Erickson Hypnotic Techniques*, vol. 2).

frontier. By simply shifting to another representational system, one that is rarely used consciously during the "waking state," a wide range may be opened for the processing of unexplored frontiers, new concepts, new beliefs, and entire alternate realities.

It is not uncommon for therapists to utilize guided visual imagery in the course of treatment. With the awareness of representational systems, it becomes obvious that to a person who has favored a visual representational system in the conscious "waking" state, guided visual fantasy may provide limited space for innovation. For such a person alternative channels such as auditory (verbal) forms of therapy, kinesthetic forms (Feldenkrais, Tai-Chi), or simply kinesthetic language or metaphor may be far more useful. The reverse is also true. Someone whose usual conscious, "waking" state representational system is kinesthetic would find visual guided imagery as incredibly powerful and useful. What constitutes an altered state of consciousness for one person might be the usual state of consciousness for another.

## Two Major Schools of Clinical Hypnosis

It would be helpful to bring to the attention of the newcomer to the field that hypnosis and the study of altered states of consciousness is a historical phenomenon. It comes to us through many cultures and many epistemologies, not just one. As a result, there are almost as many theories of hypnosis as there are authors in the field.

In terms of the current state of the art it would also be helpful to point out to the newcomer that there appear to be two major schools of thought. The first group claims that not everyone is hypnotizable. The key variable is the existence of a "trance capacity" within the subject. The second group takes the position that everyone is hypnotizable. The key variable is the skill and flexibility of the therapist.

It makes it much easier to approach the literature with these two positions in mind. Since positive results seem to come from both schools of thought, it is far more practical to consider both of them as operational models that serve useful purposes in appropriate frames of reference, rather than to think that one is true and the other is false.

Notable researchers and clinicians who exemplify the first school of thought include Herbert Spiegel, M.D., Ernest Hilgard, Ph.D., and Josephine R. Hilgard, Ph.D., to name a few. An excellent representative of the second school of thought is Milton H. Erickson, M.D.

It is highly recommended when exploring an area in which the last word has not been written that utility and clinical applicability be given priority over the search for absolute truth. Let me hasten to add that I am in favor of the discovery of absolute truth; but in the field of hypnosis absolute truth may not be forthcoming for several lifetimes. Still we can work effectively prior to its discovery. The human race used fire for thousands of years before understanding the chemistry of combustion.

With these considerations in mind we can be practical with respect to the above two schools of thought. For purposes of abbreviation, we will refer to the first school as "hypnotizability" and to the second school as "maximum flexibility."

Maximum flexibility is directly related to maximum power. By way of illustration, the only thing that differentiates the queen on the chessboard, the most powerful piece, from other pieces on the chessboard is that it has a wider range of choices. (More will be said on this subject in Chapter 6.)

To illustrate further, if a hypnotist of the "hypnotizability" school were driving a car on a road covered with oil, and the car skidded off the road and hit a tree, that hypnotist would say, "some roads are simply not drivable." If a hypnotist of the "maximum flexibility" school were driving a car down the same road, skidded off the same road, and hit a tree, such a hypnotist would say, "I am going back to that road and learn to drive on oil." Even though this sort of hypnotist may still continue to skid off the road, a great deal will be learned each time.

There is utility in each school of thought; there are advantages and disadvantages to each school of thought. An awareness of these two schools can allow a proper sequencing of the two for useful and comprehensive training. The hypnotizability school has great advantages for one just entering the field. This is not to say that those practicing within this paradigm are newcomers, but, on the contrary, here we find some of the finest and most experienced researchers and clinicians in the psychological sciences. What is being emphasized here is that, in addition to a wealth of material, one of the by-products of their work is a methodology so simple and elegant that a beginner can learn the minimum level of clinical hypnosis as outlined earlier in an amazingly short period of time.

Given the notion of hypnotizability, that is, that some people simply cannot be hypnotized, it would follow then that a test could be devised to discern between the hypnotizable and the nonhypnotizable. Many such tests have in fact been devised, including the Stanford Hypnotic Clinical

Scale (SHCS), the Harvard Group Scale of Hypnotic Susceptibility, and Spiegel's Hypnotic Induction Profile.

For the purposes of discussion, the Hypnotic Induction Profile[5] will be utilized to make a few points. It is basically a test of hypnotizability that takes approximately 10 minutes; at the end of which time the hypnotist can discern the hypnotizability of the client on a scale of zero to five. Zero is nonhypnotizable, and 20% of the clients score as nonhypnotizable. The test procedure itself involves an arm-levitation induction.

The advantages of this approach or technique are enormous for the beginner. First of all, the procedure does not take long. Since it is a test of the client's capacity, not the skill of the hypnotist, one is off to a good start. The protocol involves a very explicit script that not only includes exactly what to say, but exactly what to do. Not much time in formal instruction is required, and the technique can be mastered rather rapidly. There appears to be some correlation between nonhypnotizability on the Hypnotic Induction Profile and severe disturbance of attention. Some of those disturbances include the kind of pathological states that are rarely ever seen in the outpatient setting. Therefore, even though Spiegel's findings of hypnotizability in the general population amount to 80%, in clinical practice, since most severe states are less common in the outpatient psychotherapeutic setting, the practitioner might find that well over 90% of clients tested in the office are hypnotizable.

Once practitioners screen out the nonhypnotizable group from those with whom they will work, the client population is then exclusively hypnotizable and responsive to the simple induction procedure found in the Hypnotic Induction Profile itself. For the sophisticated beginner this has enormous value. It permits the beginner to move up quickly to the level of formulating therapeutic strategy, since one need not be overly delayed by technical considerations of trance induction and trance resolution.

The second school of hypnosis, maximum flexibility, has its advantages as well. This is the school that goes back to the oil slick road and attempts to learn to drive on it. It faces the unknown as exciting. It holds problems

[5]The emphasis in this chapter is to lightly acquaint the newcomer to hypnosis. It is necessary to point out that the applications of the Hypnotic Induction Profile for diagnosis, selection of treatment, personality assessment and research are clearly presented in Herbert Spiegel and David Spiegel, *Trance and Treatment* (New York: Basic Books, Inc., 1978). This work is indispensable to the scientific study of hypnosis and should be read by any serious student of the field.

and failures as challenges and opportunities to become masterful. The emphasis is more on operating principles than on strict procedure.

Practitioners of the hypnotizability school may also claim to utilize such operating principles. In fact, they do. The distinction can be found in that the principles used in the school of maximum flexibility would be used by the hypnotizability school only with hypnotizable subjects. Nothing could be more reasonable and consistent. However, in the other paradigm of maximum flexibility, where the emphasis is on the limits of the practitioner and not on the limits of the client, the operating principles are applied until the *practitioner* reaches a limit and cannot go any further.

Fortunately, one does not have to choose between the two schools; they are complementary. Just like two books on the same shelf, each one is complete in itself, each one a resource to the practitioner.

## HYPNOTIC COMMUNICATION

### Operating Principles

#### *Flexibility*

Here are some of the operating principles. First, there is the principle of structured flexibility itself. Translated into action it would be "if you are doing something in a communication system that is not working, don't do more of what you are doing. Instead, do *anything* else." Of course, if your "anything else" is not working, simply do "anything else." The Ericksonian or "flexibility" approach can provide the therapist with the necessary resources to afford the luxury of goal-oriented therapy. With the operational emphasis on variety of methods and the willingness to shift from one to the other, you can reach a given goal through, over, and around great obstacles.

#### *Pacing and Leading*

Given clear goals, the hypnotist then utilizes principles of goal attainment. One of the most useful of these is known as "pacing and leading."

In order to utilize this principle you need to have two points clearly demarcated. You need to know (1) where you are now and (2) where you wish to go. In other words, you need your present location and your destination. In terms of hypnosis you need to know the current immediate state of the client and the desired state. Working with the principle of *meeting clients in their model of the world*, one simply directs communication to the current state and gently moves to the desired state.

An example of this would be the following. Let us say that the desired state is relaxation. What is referred to as "leading" would be any of the hypnotist's remarks concerning relaxation. What would be referred to as "pacing" would be any of the hypnotist's remarks that describe the current state of the client that are *easily verifiable by the client.*[6,7]

Therefore, with the client sitting in a comfortable chair, his or her arms on the armrest, the hypnotist might make the following five statements. Statements 1 through 4 would constitute pacing, statement 5 would constitute leading:

1. And you are sitting in that chair.
2. And your arms are on the armrest.
3. And your feet are on the floor.
4. And you're breathing in and out (corresponding to actual inhalation and exhalation).
5. And you are relaxing more and more.

The idea is a simple one, and an effective one. Meet the client in the client's model of the world, and then go in the desired direction. No matter how desirable the goal is and no matter how appropriate it would be for personal fulfillment of the client, as long as the goal exists outside of the client's model of the world (or has been communicated to the client without the pacing step), the therapist remains alone with the idea.

## Use of Language

The use of language in hypnotic communication is both an art and a skill. It is learnable and has many interesting dimensions. Milton H. Erickson is well known for his mastery of the use of language in effective hypnotic

---

[6]The reader can find a great deal of highly valuable material, not only on pacing and leading, but on many other structures of hypnotic communication in R. Bandler and J. Grinder, *Patterns of the Hypnotic Techniques of Milton H. Erickson, M.D.*, vol. 1 (Cupertino, CA: Meta Publications, 1975) (hereafter cited as *Erickson Hypnotic Techniques*, vol. 1), and Grinder, DeLozier, and Bandler, *Erickson Hypnotic Techniques*, vol. 2.

[7]Bandler and Grinder, *Erickson Hypnotic Techniques*, vol. 1, pp. 14–25.

communication. It is no wonder that books have been written about his work, by himself as well as others, focusing explicitly on this point, and it is further no wonder that one of the best expositions of Ericksonian communication would come from the collaboration of a theoretician of psychological process with a professor of linguistics, namely, Richard Bandler and John Grinder.[8–10]

## *Transderivational Search*

Utilizing the concept of transderivational search from the field of linguistics, Bandler and Grinder propose a model of hypnotic communication.[11] Stated simply, whatever words are used overtly in communication, the unconscious mind scans for choices of meaning. Some words can have three or four meanings. Some sentences can be taken in a multiplicity of ways. While one meaning might be available to the conscious mind, the other meanings are all available simultaneously to the unconscious mind. Intelligent use of this principle can produce results hypnotically.

Given that the key element in pacing is that the hypnotist delivers verifiable descriptions of the client's experience, Erickson frequently uses nonspecific words eliciting a transderivational search on the part of the subject so that the subject seemingly verifies what the hypnotist claims. Erickson might say, "You are sitting in that chair and *experiencing certain sensations on your back*." The term "certain sensations" refers to experiences that the hypnotist could not possibly have any idea about. Yet it sounds very specific to say "certain sensations." The transderivational search on the part of the subject causes the subject to locate a certain sensation. Upon finding some sensation in the back, the subject has the experience that the hypnotist knows about the sensation. It is "verified."

Erickson is a master of this form of communication. The simple aware-

---

[8]Ibid.

[9]Grinder, DeLozier, and Bandler, *Erickson Hypnotic Techniques*, vol. 2.

[10]Some of Erickson's writing on this subject can be found in Jay Haley, ed., *Advanced Techniques of Hypnosis and Therapy* (New York: Grune & Stratton, 1967), pp. 515–520. A wealth of material for students can be found in Milton H. Erickson, E. L. Rossi, and S. I. Rossi, *Hypnotic Realities* (New York: Irvington Publishers, Inc., 1976). The two-volume series of Bandler and Grinder cited earlier are unprecedented in the clarity and structural validity of Erickson's work.

[11]Bandler and Grinder, *Erickson Hypnotic Techniques*, vol. 1, pp. 217–231.

ness of this principle can raise the performance skill of the hypnotist enormously.

## Distraction of the Conscious Mind and Utilization of the Unconscious

In addition, there is the principle of distraction of the conscious mind, and utilization of the unconscious mind.[12] This appears classically in those inductions in which the hypnotist has the subject gaze at a candle or watch and, by appropriate pacing and leading, guides the subject into an altered state of consciousness. The candle and watch serve the purpose of fixating attention and distracting the conscious mind.

Here it would be useful to recall the value of working with the unconscious mind. If one believes that the unconscious mind is the seat of primitive, destructive power and that it should rightfully be held under lock and key, and further that such control is the job of the conscious mind, then the distraction of the conscious mind and the utilization of the unconscious mind appears to be no more and no less than a dangerous mistake. Actual work in this area shows that nothing could be farther from the truth. In fact it is always gratifying to experience the fundamental ingenuity, problem-solving capabilities, efficacy, and grace of the unconscious mind. The storehouse of untold human resources reside in its realm and are quite remarkably available upon request. Recognizing that the unconscious mind is not someone or something else than a part of the person, one can provide great service at the right moment and under appropriate circumstances by distracting the conscious mind and utilizing the resources of the unconscious mind.

## Overt and Covert Channels

This brings us to the subject of overt and covert communication. Almost everyone is familiar with overt hypnotic communication. This is usually portrayed in caricature style by the classic hypnotist found in movies and television. Directions are overt and explicit; commands are done in a domineering fashion; there is really nothing subtle about the process what-

---

[12]Ibid., pp. 137–203.

soever. This is the way hypnosis is usually presented to the uninformed. It is commonly thought of as the only approach. Here again, Erickson provides us with an alternative. By simply observing *normal* communication in others, Erickson observed the ubiquitous use of covert communication. He also observed that this covert communication was delivered through unconscious channels of both the sender and receiver. Despite the lack of conscious awareness of the communication, responses were elicited in the receiver. Erickson simply adapted this finding to the field of hypnosis and with conscious intent directed messages through these covert pathways. His work abounds in this form of communication. In the hands of the skilled practitioner, it is gentle, elegant, and highly effective. One example of covert communication would be the use of embedded commands. By placing a certain tonal emphasis on key words in a sentence, Erickson observed that those words would be taken unconsciously as though they were a separate statement.

THERAPIST [*overt command*]: You will now sit quietly and relax.

ERICKSON: I wonder if you ever thought about what it might feel like to *sit quietly and relax*.

Erickson has not directly asked the subject to perform the desired response; yet, he *has*—indirectly. The unconscious mind picks this up and the subject sits quietly and relaxes.

One of my favorite quotes from Erickson's work involves his shifting of future tense into present tense in a single sentence with an embedded command. By use of the future tense the conscious mind is distracted, leaving no need for resistance; this is then followed by the embedded command in the present tense:

ERICKSON: When next I say the word "now" you will close your eyes, *now*.

If one is in rapport at that point, it is difficult to keep the eyes open.

Pacing and leading in hypnotic communication is assisted by the use of certain connective words, such as the conjunction "and."[13] For example, "*and* you are sitting in the chair, *and* breathing in and out, *and* relaxing more and more."

---

[13]Ibid., p. 147.

## Building or Dissolving Beliefs

Given the linguistic capacity to move the client from experience to experience, one can gently move from the possible to the probable to the actual. By adding increments of certainty at each level, one moves more and more toward the desired state. The following is an excerpt from such a hypnotic communication:

> [*hypnotist placing the arm in an outstretched position*]
>
> See if you can imagine your arm to be something like a lead pipe, firmly outstretched in space. I know it is not a pipe, but try to imagine.

Now that possibilities have been created in terms of imagining or pretending, the hypnotist moves more to the realm of the probable.

> And now that you can imagine your arm as a lead pipe, begin to feel the feelings as if your arm were stiff, made out of lead, totally out of your usual control, and getting stiffer and stiffer while you comfortably notice and watch it from a distance inward.

While the hypnotist is monitoring the responses of the subject, he has now moved into the realm of the probable and begins to go to the actual.

> And now your arm *is* comfortably, rigidly still, it *is* unable to move, it cannot move, try as hard as you can, you cannot move it.

At this point, receptive subjects find themselves unable to move their arms. Conceptually, the movement has been from the possible to the actual.

The hypnotist, continuing with such overt commands, can have the option at that point to cancel the command abruptly by stating "your arm is now completely normal, you can relax your arm." This approach relies on the creation of actuality in the channel of the communication itself. Whatever this hypnotist says is now a statement of actuality, including the cancelation of the original command.

If such cancelation is desired, the hypnotist also has the choice to move more fluidly in the reverse direction, from actuality to probability to possibility, by introducing the element of doubt. For example,

> Even though your arm is now absolutely stiff, I'm not sure [*doubt*] whether it must remain that way. In fact, I don't know [*doubt*] if it's beginning to

> relax and might in fact be doing that more and more at this point [*possibility of returning to the normal*] and, in fact, it's quite possible when I count to three, your arm will feel quite as comfortable as before and be totally back under your control as usual. One, two, three.

Using a bit of imagination, the reader can appreciate that the above example of the change in relationship of self to arm is generalizable to areas more central to psychotherapy.

Using the escalation of certainty through possibility, probability, and actuality, reality and belief systems can be created with hypnotic communication. By introducing doubt, reality and beliefs can be gently dissolved in hypnotic communication.

Language is not the only way to communicate hypnotically. While developing skills in this area, one can also explore the realm of nonverbal communication.

## Nonverbal Marking

Nonverbal marking is an area of study and of skill that is discussed in a variety of literature. It runs through the study of kinesics, the literature of body language. It can also be found in both the hypnosis literature ("cues" and posthypnotic "signals") and the literature of classical conditioning. It is also highly developed as a multifaceted technique in the field of neurolinguistic programming under the term "anchoring."[14]

For the purposes of this discussion we will highlight a few points. If a naturally occurring behavior or experience is artificially synchronized to an external stimulus by the process of association, and if that same external stimulus occurs at another point in time, the same natural behavior or experience may be elicited. This is a highly useful finding.

It is a phenomenon that does not require the artificial atmosphere of the laboratory or the office. For example, it is a common experience to hear a song played on the radio that is reminiscent of a special summer many years ago. As the song plays, one relives the experience. The response

[14]One of the best descriptions of anchoring can be found in Leslie C. Bandler, *They Lived Happily Ever After* (Cupertino, CA: Meta Publications, 1978), pp. 102–126.

can be so automatic and compelling that, even though the conscious and voluntary mind prefers not to relive the experience, the irresistible quality of the link between song and summer experience prevails.

Erickson utilized this phenomenon to mark out several channels for multiple message communication. He discovered that he could send two or even three messages to the subject at any given time, interspersing the messages within what seems to be a single statement. By placing message number one in a slightly higher tone of voice, message number two in a middle range tonality, and message number three in a low tone, he was capable of clearly marking the channels and sending three coherent messages to the unconscious at the same time.

The process of marking a given experience with an associated stimulus provides a powerful degree of communication leverage. Rather than being limited by the possibly random quality of normal communication, the therapist can instead become a more effective guide in therapeutic communication. Just as a guide in a tour of a city effectively points out to the tourist exactly what is being presented at the given moment by gesture, location, and so on, the therapist can intentionally and with success move the client from one experience to another with purpose and with intention, by marking with associated stimuli.

The knowledge alone that one can introduce a stimulus that brings out a specific response opens the gate to the use of it, or to the elimination of the misuse of it. One example of the misuse of an "anchor" or such a special stimulus–response link would be found in the treatment of some "chronically depressed" individuals.

There are some clients being misdiagnosed as chronically depressed merely because whenever they are sitting in the therapist's consulting room they are depressed. It is important to ask such a client what the experience was just prior to coming into the office. It is quite possible that the client was in a relatively good mood prior to walking into the office, and upon arriving in the waiting room the simple association of the interior of the waiting room with previous sessions of depression had at least as potent an effect as did the song as a reminder of the summer. In other words, the good mood is displaced since the office itself has been linked to the client's previous emotional climate in that setting. The client becomes depressed, and then enters the consulting room.

This is not to say that all chronic depression is caused by simple stimulus–response to previous unhappy therapeutic sessions. However, with this awareness the therapist can inquire as to the client's state just prior to coming into the office and differentiate one group from the other. Such is an example of a misuse or an inadvertent negative use of naturally occurring anchors.

As a useful tool of psychotherapy, anchoring becomes the firmly attached link between an experience in the world of the client and the responsible hands of the therapist. The channel for the stimulus can be any of the sensory channels—visual, auditory, kinesthetic, olfactory, gustatory. An anchor is not simply a stimulus. An anchor is a stimulus that reliably reproduces a specific response.

Let us return to the "chronically depressed" client, who was not truly depressed but unfortunately anchored negatively to seeing the office. The therapist inquires as to how the client was feeling just prior to coming into the office. The client responds with positive affect, a smile on the face, saying, "I was in a pretty good mood." If the therapist, at the peak moment of positive affect, introduces a stimulus, a gesture, a touch, a sound, then an anchor to the *positive* feeling might be established. The therapist will know that the anchor has been established if making the same gesture results in the same positive affect in the client. Intelligent use of the positive anchor can cancel the effects of the previous negative anchor.

Anchoring is frequently taught in introductory neurolinguistic programming workshops as a kinesthetic stimulus—usually a touch on the shoulder or arm. In more advanced work one learns that anchoring can be done via any sensory channel, including words. Essentially, you know you have an anchor if you can demonstrate the response it should elicit. For the therapist an anchor is a handle on the client's world. It is a way to summon forth experience or behavior.

Anchors are usually used in the following three functions: integration, separation, and sequencing.

### *Integration*

Frequently, presenting problems take the following form. A client responds in an uncomfortable way to some particular setting. The client desires a better response to that setting. Furthermore, the desired way of responding may actually be available to the client in some other setting in life. In other words, it is as though, in a given context, a person does not have access to resources that they already possess.

For example, a person might wish to have "confidence" in a particular setting. However, they experience anxiety. Yet, they do experience "confidence" somewhere else. There are many approaches to this problem, ranging all the way from the pharmacologic to the psychoanalytic.

Anchoring also can be used. The therapist has the client return to a time, perhaps with eyes closed, in memory, when the desired resource "confidence" was experienced. The client then develops that resource experientially to the fullest, and at its peak point signals the therapist, perhaps by a nod of the head. The therapist quickly touches the client, arbitrarily, on the *left* shoulder. The therapist might then test the anchor by touching the shoulder again and noticing whether it brings forth the desired response, "confidence."

Having established the anchor for the desired response, the therapist asks the client to return experientially, perhaps with eyes closed, to the setting in which the response is desired, and in which the negative undesired response appears. When the person evidences externally the negative affect, and validates this with his or her own internal response, the therapist anchors the situation that calls up a negative experience, perhaps with a touch on the *right* shoulder.

Now we have an anchor for the situation that is a natural anchor for a negative state (right shoulder) and an anchor for the positive resource (left shoulder). Since these touches will bring forth the experiences—a Pavlovian link, if you will—the therapist can directly introduce a shift at this point. It can be done with grace and elegance if appropriate accompanying words are synchronized with the nonverbal signals:

> [*therapist touches right shoulder*]
> Recall that situation in which you had that bad experience.
> [*patient evidences negative affect*]
>
> [*therapist, while holding the anchor on the right shoulder*]
> Good. Now bring all those positive resources
> [*touches left shoulder while holding the right shoulder*]
> into this situation, and notice the result.

By triggering both anchors, the therapist introduces integration into the system, nonverbally, while supporting actions with words.

### *Separation*

In addition, the use of anchoring provides an opportunity to separate experiences that have unfortunately been linked in an unwanted manner. Clinical examples of such links occur most noticeably in psychological trauma and phobia. (In phobia the *sight* of the phobic object may be linked to a powerful internal *feeling* of fear.)

Descriptions of the use of anchoring to separate links of experience are found in the neurolinguistic programming literature under the heading V–K Dissociation.[15]

### *Sequencing*

Anchoring can be used to arrange experience in a given sequence so that a given stimulus will produce an orderly set of sequenced responses. This is highly useful in the process of learning as well as in therapy. Simply consider any complicated piece of behavior, such as typing, driving a car, the martial arts, and so on. A given stimulus results (in the trained individual) in a sequence of appropriate behaviors or experiences.

This type of work is found in abundance in the writings and videotapes of Erickson. It is also clearly elucidated under "strategy elicitation" and "installation" in the neurolinguistic programming literature, to which the reader is referred for details.[16]

For our purposes here it is useful to appreciate that it is not only possible, but also desirable, to be able to summon forth, via anchoring, a given resource of the client at an appropriate and useful time. The client's resources are available upon request. Anchoring can be thought of as an indexing system for calling upon the desired resources. It is a natural phenomenon and can be used by the therapist, by the client, or by both.

Many of these skills, including anchoring, have the advantage of leverage. For example, if you want to find a specific book in a library that has a collection of hundreds of thousands of volumes, and you are unfamiliar with the indexing system and how to employ the services of the

---

[15]Ibid., pp. 117–124. This is highly recommended.

[16]R. Dilts, J. Grinder, R. Bandler, L. C. Bandler, and J. DeLozier *Neuro-Linguistic Programming*, vol. 1 (Cupertino, CA: Meta Publications, 1980).

trained librarian, the search for your book will be a nightmare of insurmountable processing. Once you become aware of the indexing system and the availability of professional assistance, the matter becomes highly simplified. The emphasis then is upon what is being retrieved, rather than whether or not you can find the work at all.

Similarly, anchoring permits the practitioner to work directly with the integration, separation, and sequencing of behavior and experience. Therapeutic considerations become more sophisticated, such as what to integrate, what to separate, and what to sequence, rather than whether it can really be done in the first place.

## METAPHOR

Metaphor is one of the most delightful techniques found in hypnotic and therapeutic communication. Put simply, it is the technique of storytelling. It was one of the favorite techniques of Erickson who used it extensively throughout his work. David Gordon has written an excellent work in which he details not only the analysis of the method itself, but also clearly presents how to do it.[17]

For our purposes here it is worthwhile to present only some of the salient features of this modality. To begin with, it is a method that evokes little or no resistance. The therapist is in the role of storyteller and the listener is simply paying attention to the material found in the story. The story is about someone or something else other than the listener, and if it is told in an interesting and delightful or provocative manner, the listener is easily engaged in the process.

A reader can easily become identified with characters in a story or a play. In the therapeutic use of storytelling, the therapist, aware of this, structures the story so that it is relevant to the given problem and also structures possible solutions within the story. Consciously, clients pay attention to the details of the story. Unconsciously, by means of transderivational search, clients find relevance and applicability to their own situations.

This method has been known for centuries and is found in many cul-

---

[17]David Gordon, *Therapeutic Metaphors* (Cupertino, CA: Meta Publications, 1978).

tures. It predates the written word; it originated when cultures relied solely on the spoken tradition. The sophisticated therapist, aware of the power and efficacy of this method, will find reviewing ancient religious myths and stories, particularly those that had strict rules regarding their transcribing, extremely rewarding.

A few examples will suffice. Let us say, for purposes of illustration, that the desired response in the client is relaxation. Using the information mentioned earlier in this chapter, one might use pacing and leading with direct instruction for relaxation. On the other hand, one might use anchoring. Invite the individual to recall a time when he or she was appropriately relaxed, anchor it, and trigger the anchor. One might use embedded commands.

In addition, one can use metaphor.

One could tell a story about someone else, a story with appropriate sequencing, that, if followed by the reader or listener, could easily induce a state of relaxation.

> Once there was a man whose life was very difficult. He would wake up early in the morning to go to work in the fields. He would do backbreaking labor; by the time the midday sun came into its fullest, baking down great heat, he would discover little time for lunch, let alone to satisfy his need for water. Chronically hot and thirsty, he would put in a full day's work until sundown, when he would return to the house. That was the very special part of the day that he always looked forward to and yearned for; because when he would enter that house, the fresh aroma of baked bread, the bubbling sound of the food being cooked on the stove would begin to fill him with delight. What meant the most to him, strange as it may seem, was the sound of the water rushing into his bathtub, announcing to him in its own special way, an invitation for deep relaxation. As pleasure would begin to spread across his face, the only thing that could offer him more would be his actually stepping into the tub, lying down, closing his eyes, and permitting his body to be supported, covered by the soothing and comfortable water, without any effort whatsoever on his part.

If one tells a story such as this to a client emphasizing key words and phrases, one might well notice relaxation, similar to that described in the story, beginning to appear in the client. The trained communicator pays attention to the client straight through the story and notices the observable cues showing that the client is, in fact, responding. For example, when describing the heat and brilliance and the sunshine, if the client's eyelids begin to blink as though the sun were very bright in the room, one has an indication that the client has identified with the character in the story.

Erickson used this technique for a multitude of purposes, including pain control.[18,19] In an actual case, Erickson worked with a florist named Joe, who was suffering from a terminal malignancy. By telling this florist a story about a tomato plant feeling "comfortable and peaceful," the patient began to experience relief. This gem is now a classic.

Erickson adds another dimension to storytelling by the use of sequencing. Just as one can use the notion of sequence in utilization of the technique of anchoring, one can also sequence stories.

The above example of the man working in the field has within it a *sequence* of experiences that builds naturally from tension toward relaxation. All these experiential states are contained within one story. It is also possible to sequence these states by telling separate stories, each involving one state, and sequencing these stories. The relaxation produced may be the same.

The advantage in the separate story technique is the further reduction of resistance. Since each story may be totally unrelated to the next with respect to content and totally unrelated with respect to the experiences evoked in one with those evoked in another, then the only link is the sequence. Unless the client is aware of this technique, there is almost no way for the client to be consciously aware of this channel of communication. The result is maximal delivery of the message.

Let me hasten to add that the unconscious mind is also the seat of our deepest defenses. Moreover, it is the utilization of the material by the unconscious mind that gives us the desired therapeutic result. If the message delivered by the well-intentioned therapist through minimal conscious resistance is in any way perceived by the unconscious mind as unwelcome input, it is likely to be rejected by the client.

The purpose of this chapter is to present to the reader major areas of study and skill to be acquired. Clearly to have such communication technique as part of one's repertoire is a decided advantage. The problems our clients bring to us are difficult enough as it is. The extent to which we can make our own efforts more effective, graceful, and fluid will determine how profoundly we can assist our clients toward their specified goals.

---

[18]Haley, *Techniques of Hypnosis*, pp. 515–520.

[19]Bandler and Grinder, *Erickson Hypnotic Techniques*, vol. 1, pp. 26–50.

The subject of human communication, in particular the subject of hypnosis and hypnotic communication, is so fascinating and seductively intriguing that it is possible for the newcomer to the field to get stuck on this level, and many people do. For training purposes it is even recommended that the newcomer stay at this level long enough to achieve basic mastery of the construction of metaphorical stories, the utilization of anchoring, and the induction and resolution of a hypnotic trance state.

It must be emphasized, however, that, although this material is necessary to the work of a good transformational psychotherapy, it is not sufficient. The best one can hope to achieve mastering these techniques is to become a master technician. A great stonemason is not an architect.

It is in utilization and proper application of these communication skills that one distinguishes therapist from technician. The remainder of this book will focus upon those key elements of strategy and purpose that have relevance to areas beyond technique.

Discussion at such a level is far from new in the field of psychology. The dilemma for the practitioner of psychotherapy is usually not on the level of a paucity of good ideas and formulations of problems and solutions. The dilemma is usually on the level of what to do about them.

The techniques of rapport and hypnotic communication presented in these last two chapters are examples of some of the powerful methods that have begun to emerge. Some are ancient, some are derivative of the ancient, and some might be brand new. The scientific revolution has taken us away from many useful and effective methods that lasted through hundreds of thousands of years of human development. They were refined by evolution, by survival of the fittest, a principle applicable to ideas as well as species. We are now in an era that is recovering what was lost in our haste during the past few hundred years, not to negate our progress, but to integrate our powerful heritage with our new findings. Translated into psychotherapy, these "new/old" techniques enable us to be at least as skillful doers as we are thinkers.

The reader is strongly encouraged to obtain training in the above skills as soon as possible. The rest of this book focuses on levels of strategy and purpose. I am sure that these subsequent chapters can be understood easily on an intellectual level. When actual skill has been acquired in the above areas of technique, even on an elementary level, the subsequent chapters will have enormous personal value and relevance, far beyond what one can initially perceive on first reading.

CHAPTER

# 4

# KEY OPERATIONAL COMPONENTS

The last two chapters have dealt with some basic building blocks of effective and purposeful communication.

This chapter and the next will deal with matters on a totally different level. Given the communication skills of the previous two chapters, what separates the technician from the technically skilled psychotherapist are issues on the level of strategy, purpose, and design. This is the kind of distinction that separates the master carpenter from the architect. The architect cannot achieve the actualization of his design without the skill of the master carpenter. Likewise, the master carpenter is limited without the creative and practical design of the architect. As we proceed from realm to realm, it is useful to appreciate that first, mastery is encouraged within the given realm, and second, we must be aware when we shift to the next realm.

This section deals with issues of strategy and design. Given the skill of the previous chapters and the abundance rather than the scarcity of such powerful communication techniques, the issue then becomes one of strategic organization of efforts to achieve desired goals.

If there is any one principle that cannot be emphasized too much throughout this book, it is the principle of maximum flexibility. The keystone to efficacy is the willingness to stay on course if the course is productive, and the willingness to shift course immediately if it is not. The investment remains in the goal, not in the method.

In this chapter a sample of six key components have been selected for presentation. This is not to imply that there are only six such elements in existence. On the contrary, these six constitute a minimum of such constructs that should be readily available to the practitioner. After these six components have been mastered, it is not only feasible but advantageous as well for the clinician to find or create new ones to add to the list. Incidentally, the most exciting contexts in which to create new operations are precisely those in which the following six components are not evidencing results:

1. Reframing
2. Learning Sets
3. Motivation (positive and negative)
4. TOTE
5. Recontextualization
6. Awareness of Self as Context

These six components are absolutely not related in a linear fashion. They simply coexist conceptually, like different books on the same shelf or different rooms in the same apartment. Each has a separate purpose and function unrelated to the other on the level of that function. They are related, however, in that they are conceptual tools of the therapist. In fact, the only connection among the various books on a shelf may very well be the person who reads them.

Take each component for itself. Consider each one as a resource. Your imagination is encouraged to seek out applicability beyond whatever clinical examples are indicated.

## REFRAMING

The term *reframing* appears in various places in the literature and with different meanings. The term as presented here refers specifically to the six-step model of Bandler and Grinder.[1] It is a marvelous concise formula. One could even say that these should be the six steps of any complete psychotherapy. The six steps lie outside of any specific method. It is this

---

[1]Leslie C. Bandler, *They Lived Happily Ever After* (Cupertino, CA: Meta Publications, 1978), pp. 127–142.

advantage that permits the therapist—from psychoanalyst to psychodramatist—to utilize reframing wherever deemed appropriate *within* the existing methodology.

Interestingly enough, if the existing method happens to be hypnosis, then the utilization of reframing by means of direct communication with the unconscious mind can result in profound transformational effect as a result of a single session. Although formal studies have not yet been done, clinical experience definitely supports this statement.

As presented by Bandler and Grinder, the six steps are as follows:

1. Identify the pattern you wish to change.
2. Establish communication with the part responsible for that pattern.
3. Separate pattern from intention.
4. Obtain new satisfying ways to serve the above intention.
5. Have the part responsible ratify the new ways.
6. Perform an ecological check.

Although the reader is referred to the neurolinguistic programming literature,[2] an overview might be helpful.

This is a sequence that, when processed by means of hypnosis, functions on two levels. Step 1 utilizes participation of the conscious mind. Steps 2 through 6 involve operations of the unconscious mind.

Since the unconscious mind is always present and operating, it naturally participates even if the therapist is unaware of this fact or is not intending to utilize the unconscious mind. Therefore one can have options regarding the extent of participation of the *conscious* mind in this process.

When reframing is used as a model in standard psychotherapy, consciousness may be brought into play in steps 2 through 6. For our purposes here the six steps will be presented within hypnotherapy, demonstrating the use of the unconscious directly for steps 2 through 6. In addition, there will be some allusion to the analogous steps in analytic therapy and psychodrama to highlight the conviction that reframing need not be thought of as a "technique" but rather as a model or strategy to be implemented within the therapeutic modality of your choice.

---

[2]R. Dilts, J. Grinder, R. Bandler, L. C. Bandler, and J. DeLozier, *Neuro-Linguistic Programming*, vol. 1 (Cupertino, CA: Meta Publications, 1980).

Naturally, the depth of comparison between the modalities will remain on just the level necessary to make the point. In-depth comparative analysis must await its own volume.

## Step One: Identify the Pattern

While not yet in a hypnotic trance, and with full utilization of the conscious mind, the client is asked to identify the pattern (behavior, experience, sequence) that is to be changed. The equivalent in most mainstream psychotherapies is identifying a "chief complaint" or a "presenting problem." Naturally, in a verbal psychotherapy one would expect explicit description of this problem.

In a hypnotherapy, however, there is the additional option to proceed in a contentless manner. For purposes of communication the client is asked to name or label the pattern with a code name, letter, or number. It really does not matter what the label is as long as the vocalization of the label functions to retrieve in memory the pattern that it stands for. The label could be thought of as a verbal anchor or index for the pattern. Once the pattern has been identified, the following steps are executed, usually in an altered state of consciousness and usually with ideomotor signals for "yes" and for "no" from the unconscious mind.

The use of ideomotor signaling is as old as the field of hypnosis itself. For the newcomer to the field, suffice it to say that with a person in a hypnotic trance state it is possible to obtain nonverbal cues from the unconscious mind that are absolutely consistent and clinically reliable for affirmation ("yes") and negation ("no"). An example might be an involuntary movement of the left index finger for "yes" and an involuntary movement of the right index finger for "no." Given such yes/no communication, one can easily proceed with steps 2–6. Further, let us say that the pattern to be changed has been labeled "pattern X," by the client.

## Step Two: Communicate with the Part Responsible

In a psychoanalytically oriented therapy the stage of communicating with the "part responsible" usually appears after one is well into therapy, certainly past the original identification of presenting problems (step 1).

Such communication can be achieved, for example, when a vivid memory of the origin of the symptom surfaces. It is especially helpful when it is recalled in the first person and the present tense. Another opportunity to communicate with the part responsible might be when the pattern occurs in the transference and is consciously experienced by the client in the "here and now."

At such a point the pattern may not be ego-alien, and the client is then speaking *as* the "part responsible" for the pattern. (Of course, one would not label a client a "part responsible." More appropriate would be the term "person responsible.") Nevertheless, the original setting for the pattern has been recreated in memory or transferential projection. Upon reorientation to the present time/space coordinates, it is clear that the person he or she "is now" is not the same person he or she "was then" creating the symptom.

In psychodrama communication with the part responsible occurs when the protagonist reenacts the scene in which the symptom or problem emerged. In this treatment modality the person could be considered in the "role responsible" rather than the part responsible.

In either the psychoanalytic or psychodramatic setting there is usually a profound awareness of the adaptive quality or appropriateness of the symptom within the original remembered context.

In a hypnotherapy, by means of ideomotor signals within a contentless mode, communication with the part responsible becomes a brief interaction comprised of the delivery of process instructions. Furthermore, this occurs during the same session as step 1, actually in the next few moments, as follows:

CLIENT [*in a hypnotic trance state*]

HYPNOTIST: I would now like to get in communication with the part responsible for "pattern X." When I am, I will get a "yes."

CLIENT [*totally motionless. Pause. Right finger moves up, signifying "yes"*]

HYPNOTIST: And what's a signal for "no"?

CLIENT [*pause. Left finger moves up*]

## Step Three: Separate Pattern from Intention

Step 3 calls for a distinction to be made between the pattern (symptom) and the intention (adaptive function). This is a familiar step in psychotherapy. The symptom or "problem" was actually a "solution" at one time in the past. What makes it a problem now is that it is currently an *obsolete* solution. Upon analysis one frequently discovers the positive purpose it had originally served. Usually it is a purpose one would still wish served. However, what is desired is a more age-appropriate or more currently adaptive means of serving the purpose.

Making the distinction between pattern and intention opens a deeper level of choice for change. The psychoanalytic equivalent of making this distinction is to discover the cause or rationale for the symptom by precise exploration when the issue is recreated in the office, perhaps during the analysis of the specific transference reaction or relived memory. There are far too many variations in how this distinction appears in analytic practice for review in this volume.

In psychodrama similar discovery of a distinction between behavior and purpose occurs when the protagonist is in role, reenacting the original presenting problem. It is often inappropriate in psychodrama to ask "why?" since the answer (the intention) is quite obvious by the nature of the situation, that is, the enactment.

In a contentless reframing, using ideomotor signals, one can simply deliver an instruction to the "part" responsible asking "it" to make the distinction between pattern and intention, and notify the therapist by the signaling system as to when the task has been accomplished. Again, this occurs within the same single session as a "third step" as follows:

HYPNOTIST: Patterns in life tend to be created by the unconscious mind in order to serve useful and positive purposes, which I will refer to as "intention." When the part responsible for "pattern X" has distinguished between its pattern and its intention, I will get a "yes."

CLIENT [*pauses. Right finger goes up*]

## Step Four: Obtain New Patterns to Serve the Intention

Now that the distinction has been made between the unwanted pattern and the positive purpose that it serves, new alternative patterns of high quality are needed to replace the old ones. If rendered available to the part responsible, the new patterns will, ideally, serve the purpose (intention) with the desired benefit of being age-appropriate, satisfying, and so on.

The equivalent endeavor in standard outpatient psychotherapy occurs frequently during very creative sessions. Hypothetically, for example, a therapist may say, "Since you are doing this (symptom) in order to serve this particular purpose (intention) do you think that now that you are older and wiser that you can, *now*, come up with another way to serve the purpose, a way that is not so destructive to who you are at this point in your life?" If the timing is right, creativity enters the process and age-appropriate solutions may emerge quite prolifically.

The equivalent in psychodrama may occur during an impasse. While the protagonist is locked in a scene in which the presenting problem is enacted and the intention is obvious and positive, the director may have another member of the group stand in for the protagonist (a double). By this technique both protagonist and director step back from the scene far enough to get perspective on the matter. The director then asks, "Do you think there may be another way to play this scene? A more satisfying way?" In effect, the protagonist is in the role of "creative one" and often good, constructive ideas emerge. They are then tested in the scene itself until they pass the standards of both satisfaction and high adaptive quality.

In hypnosis this can be done "behind the scenes," so to speak. Without bringing the intention to consciousness, the therapist can simply request intrapsychic communication between the part responsible and a creative "part." The process is monitored with ideomotor signals. Once again, this is still within the same session as the previous steps and appears as a "fourth step" as follows:

HYPNOTIST: There is a creative part that can create ***brand-new, satisfying***, to the highest standards of the conscious mind, ***adequate***, meaning it works as well as the previous pattern ever worked, ***alternative patterns*** for any intention whatsoever. The part responsible for "pattern X" will now get in communication with that creative part. When that communication has been established, I will get a "yes."

CLIENT [*pause. Right finger goes up*]

HYPNOTIST: Good. The part responsible for "pattern X" will now communicate its intention to the creative part, and when the creative part receives it, I'll get a "yes."

CLIENT [*right finger goes up*]

HYPNOTIST: The creative part will now create three, four, five, or six new, satisfying, adequate, alternative patterns for that specific intention. And communicate these new patterns to the part responsible for "pattern X." When the part responsible for "pattern X" receives these new patterns, I'll get a "yes."

CLIENT [*some shifting of the body. Right finger goes up*]

## Step Five: Have the Part Responsible Ratify the New Patterns

Step 5 enables the very part that produced the undesirable pattern or "symptom" to be responsible for the new adaptive patterns or "cure." In many psychotherapies this usually follows the previous step. Once a person has considered new adaptive ways to serve the purpose, the therapist might ask if the client would be willing to try them out. If the person is willing, a major step has been completed. In some therapies the therapist would ask the client to do it as a "homework" assignment.

Such a behavioral experiment may rarely be directly requested in a psychoanalysis; but if the analysis is primarily for therapy rather than strictly for education the implication to try out new behavior may be there as an implied obvious next step.

In psychodrama the protagonist may be asked to test the behavior at home, having tested it in the group.

In a hypnotherapy reframing directs the communication to the unconscious mind, in particular to the part responsible for the original undesired pattern. This is a continuation of the same session as the previous steps using ideomotor signals to monitor the process, as follows:

HYPNOTIST: Now that the part responsible has received its new patterns, it can discover that these new patterns, in fact, do serve the intention at least as well as the previous pattern ever did, and that they all are highly satisfying to the conscious mind, making them, in fact, superior patterns to "pattern X." The part responsible can now take responsibility for these new patterns and agree to use them with priority. When the part responsible has taken responsibility for these new patterns I will get a "yes."

CLIENT [*multiple small body movements. Right index finger goes up*]

HYPNOTIST: Good.

## Step Six: Perform an Ecological Check

Although the part responsible has agreed to use its new patterns, the entire system beyond that specific part has not yet been taken into account. If the process stops here, one can produce what is termed in the psychoanalytic literature as an "ego-alien" change. Other aspects of the personality may demand the return of the symptom even though the part responsible for it originally was willing to let it go. This frequently is referred to as the issue of secondary gain versus primary gain. It is usually dealt with in psychotherapy by the "working-through" process.

This sixth step attempts to provide *in advance* the necessary internal, deep psychological work usually provided by the working-through process, utilizing the vast, computerlike capabilities of the human brain to anticipate, extrapolate, and adapt.

HYPNOTIST: The unconscious mind will now scan the entire system. Is there any part, anyplace, anywhere whatsoever, that objects to these changes?

CLIENT [*some eye movements noticed under the lids*]

If the client signals "yes," that there is an objection, the hypnotist returns to step 2 and establishes communication with the part objecting. The hypnotist will then sequence through steps 3, 4, 5, and 6, providing the part objecting with new patterns so that it need not object any further.

Once that has been achieved, a second ecological check must be performed to discover any objections to that second order of new patterns.

As long as there are objections, one recycles through steps 2 to 6. When there are no objections, the hypnotist exits the system.

CLIENT [*continuing to scan for objections. Some body movements.* Left *finger goes up, signifying "no"*]

HYPNOTIST: I understand that the entire system has been scanned, and that there are no objections anywhere. Is that correct?

CLIENT [*right finger goes up*]

HYPNOTIST: Has the entire system been scanned?

CLIENT [*right finger goes up*]

HYPNOTIST: Is there any part of the system that has not been scanned?

CLIENT [*left finger goes up*]

HYPNOTIST: Then it is my understanding that the part responsible for "pattern X" has agreed to use its new patterns with priority and there are no objections anywhere. Is that correct?

CLIENT [*right finger goes up*]

HYPNOTIST: Good. [*At this point, the hypnotherapeutic work is complete and the hypnotist brings the client out of the trance.*]

The above example of reframing utilized within a hypnotherapy is particularly useful for presentation here, inasmuch as this section is devoted to issues of strategy rather than hypnotic communication. The foregoing piece of work demonstrates this strategy vividly. Since the only communication between client and hypnotist is nonverbal and specific for "yes" and "no," we need not be distracted by the actual content or psychodynamics of the presenting problem. These matters *are* being taken into account. They are not neglected. They have simply been delegated to the parts of the client's mind that know about them very well. Although this communication employs the concept of "parts," and "talking to" them actually works, this is not meant to imply that such structures are "real." It is merely a useful metaphorical construct used to convey process instructions.

This excerpt of hypnotherapy allows us to see procedurally what we are emphasizing conceptually and strategically, namely, six steps of a transformational strategy. Incorporating these six steps into other forms of psychotherapy is just a matter of procedure and technique, once the judgment to use reframing has been made.

## LEARNING SETS

There are very few forms of psychotherapy that would not consider learning as an integral component of the work. One may wonder to what extent the natural capacity of the human mind to learn does function, even in pharmacological forms of treatment, where such learning is not necessarily intended by the practitioner.

One could interpret the processes of identification seen in childhood as a form of learning: the child learning to be an adult like father or mother. When something is learned, it is part of the system. It no longer needs to be supplied from an external source. The source is within.

A therapeutic change that is transient may not be as valuable as one that becomes an ongoing part of the internal system, available as a resource. Therefore the notion of learning is a highly useful one. Bringing this dimension into the therapy supports autonomy in the client and minimizes dependency.

There are many ways to learn. How people learn and the various ways that they go about doing it is the subject of a good deal of psychological research. Since this is another area in which the last word has not been written, it is useful to take a practical approach. Clinically, it is not necessary to know how all human beings learn or even how most human beings learn. All that is necessary is for the individual client to activate his or her own systems for learning at the appropriate time in the course of therapy. Thus the matter is simplified.

This method is exemplified in Erickson's work. As part of a hypnotic induction,[3] he instructs the unconscious mind that, as a child, learning the letters of the alphabet was an exceedingly difficult task; the conscious mind found it overwhelming, while the unconscious mind formed images of letters and numbers that would last a lifetime. He goes into great detail in describing the mastery of learning to read and the surprise of discovery on the part of the conscious mind that the job had been done outside its awareness.

As in much of Erickson's work, this technique serves a number of purposes at the same time. It is a reminder to the system of a *time* of profound learning, the results of which deeply changed the person's life and awareness of the world. There are few events as significant and as universal in our culture as the childhood event of learning to read. By means of transderivational search, the individual client scans for the relevance of this discourse on learning to read and write. Ultimately the connection is made to the presenting problem and to the therapy session. The message is communicated as "This is also a place to learn as well as a place of treatment. The learning is as priceless as learning to read and write."

## MOTIVATION

Overcoming inertia is an important tactical consideration. Motivational systems serve this purpose. Although the phenomenon of inertia can be utilized psychodynamically by a given personality, clinically it appears as primarily independent of psychodynamics. Inertia seems to have a stabilizer function that maintains the status quo until we are disturbed from within

---

[3]Milton H. Erickson, E. L. Rossi, and S. I. Rossi, *Hypnotic Realities* (New York: Irvington Publishers, Inc., 1976), pp. 6–8.

or from without. This is, of course, an oversimplification, but it serves the purpose of illustration.

When motivated, people will either move *toward* or *away from*. We can refer to the "moving away from" as negative and the "moving toward" as positive. Each of these directions is useful. The classical example of negative motivation is the avoidance of the "whip." The classical example of positive motivation is the "carrot" in front of the donkey.

In the neurolinguistic programming literature this topic appears under the heading of "motivational strategies."[4] By direct observation of the accessing cues, one can elicit the sequence of representational systems a client utilizes in the process of motivation. Knowing the motivational sequence affords the practitioner an advantage in that material can be communicated to the client *through* this sequence. Technically, this allows a message to be delivered and also includes the stimulation of necessary motivation to overcome inertia.

An example of another approach, derivative of Erickson's work, would be the following. Having established clearly formulated goals during a session, one assigns "homework" for the next session. The client is to return with a list of six past experiences. Three involve negative motivation, and three positive. In other words, three are events from the past in which the client overcame inertia in order to *avoid* the increasing discomfort of the status quo, not necessarily to get somewhere, but specifically to get away from somewhere.

The second set of three involve episodes from the past in which the client overcame inertia simply because the goal was so desirable. Discomfort of the status quo was not even a part of the episode. In fact, the status quo may have been quite pleasurable. The goal was simply desirable.

One of my recurrent clinical findings is that the session in which the client returns with the list of six experiences is highlighted by surprising stories of accomplishing many things during the week *between* the two sessions.

The mere process of doing the homework assignment activates the motivational systems themselves. The process of recalling these six events in itself causes an unconscious reliving of them.

---

[4]Dilts et al., *Neuro-Linguistic Programming*.

In addition, the unconscious mind seems to seek out a common denominator. Usually these six episodes are totally unrelated in any way except that these were times when the individual overcame inertia.

The work of transformational therapy involves changes in the personality and in life circumstances. Desirable as it might be in the given case, it does involve change. Moving from the status quo requires motivation. The awareness that motivation itself can also be worked with on the level of form, rather than simply content, has great implications in the hands of the skilled therapist.

## TOTE

George Miller[5] uses the term "TOTE" to describe a sequence of human behavior. It is a useful concept, particularly in therapies where the creation of new behavior is a desirable outcome. It is a concept that is further developed in the neurolinguistic programming literature.[6,7]

For our purposes, it is useful simply to highlight the following. With respect to leverage, the jump from content to form is an increase of an order of magnitude. Here, once again, such a jump is made. With respect to form, rather than content, a unit of behavior could be said to have a beginning, a middle, and an end.

In order for there to be a beginning, conditions of beginnings have to be met. In order for a middle to occur, conditions of middles need to be met. And in order for an end to occur, conditions of endings need to be met.

Each of the letters in the acronym TOTE stands for a step in the sequence of such a unit of behavior.

*T*est

*O*peration

*T*est

*E*xit

---

[5]G. A. Miller, E. Galanter, and K. Pribram, *Plans and the Structure of Behavior* (New York: Holt, Rinehart and Winston, 1960).

[6]J. Grinder, J. DeLozier, and R. Bandler, *Patterns of the Hypnotic Techniques of Milton H. Erickson, M.D.*, vol. 2 (Cupertino, CA: Meta Publications, 1977).

[7]Dilts et al., *Neuro-Linguistic Programming.*

The first T refers to the test, which indicates the necessary conditions for *beginning* the unit of behavior. If the piece of behavior were opening a door, the test would be the presence of the door and the need or desire to open it. Further analysis of "presence of the door" would reveal the conditions by which the presence is known, or "tested," such as seeing the door (visual input).

The O refers to the operation that then ensues. In this case it would be that the hand reaches out, grasps the doorknob, turns it, and opens the door.

The second T refers to the test conditions necessary to exit the system. In the case of opening a door, it might be the visual perception of an open door. This condition, "open door," having been met, is sufficient to lead us to the next step.

The E refers to the exit, meaning, to end the piece of behavior.

The awareness of this abstract unit of human behavior is a useful piece in understanding behavioral architecture. From the standpoint of therapy or repair, clients may have difficulty in any one of the above phases. They may have difficulty initiating or knowing when to initiate a certain operation. They might be able to initiate, but have certain difficulties within the operation itself. They might perform the operation well and still not know when to stop or what cue signals them to exit the system.

From the standpoint of creation of new behavior, it is useful to know the abstract form that would constitute a complete piece of work.

It is further useful to realize that, although TOTE can refer to the smallest unit of behavior, it can be applied to units of any size, as long as the sequence of "chunks" remains that of test, operation, test, exit.

## RECONTEXTUALIZATION

Another useful operational component is recontextualization. Once again, the principle of leverage is introduced.

In the next chapter we will be dealing directly with the issue of "context" in more detail. For our purposes in this section, suffice it to say that when you go to the level of context, you go to the root, the very heart of the matter.

Philosophically speaking, things in themselves are inherently neither good nor evil. We can be pleased or disappointed with them because of the way they fit into our scheme of things, that is, our frame of reference.

For example, if I wish to go to the beach, and it rains, I will call it "bad" weather. Simultaneously, the farmer down the road who has been disappointed with the unusual dry spell we had been having, jumps for joy at the first dark cloud approaching. It is neither "good" nor "bad" weather. The frame of reference or the context makes the difference.

This is common experience. It is a natural finding in everyday psychology. As Erickson demonstrates over and over, the utilization of natural findings and processes are among the most powerful. The reason is simple. Since they already occur in nature, they work.

Knowing that the context or frame of reference determines the quality of the experience enables the clinician to intervene on that level. The intervention can be implicit or explicit. In the process of reframing described earlier, the intervention can be found within the concept of the undesired behavior pattern serving a positive desirable intention.

Recontextualization has an "unlocking" effect. It allows us to move from the issues of subject matter into the issues of frame of reference. This can be liberating. A person enmeshed in disappointments can be disentangled by giving attention to the useful lessons they contain. The focus is on the value rather on the pain.

To begin developing the skill of recontextualization, it might be useful to have the following kinds of questions running through one's mind. When faced with a report of undeniable adversity in the client's life, one may wonder: "How is this useful to the client or to anyone else, for that matter. What is the lesson in this? How is this a challenge? If this challenge were overcome, what sorts of marvelous changes would take place in the personality? How does this very problem provide the most efficient gateway to positive personality transformation?"

It is very important to differentiate between a change in context from simply finding a positive element within a negative context. The expression "Every cloud has a silver lining" is an example of a positive element within a negative context.

Instead, the therapist takes on the mental set or frame of reference that these negative data *are already* in a positive context. We just have not yet discovered what that positive context is. With this set in operation, in the mind of the therapist, coupled with flexibility of approach toward goals, one can produce an abundance of exits from a stuck position.

## AWARENESS OF SELF AS CONTEXT

The previous sections dealt with issues and techniques that can be studied, learned, and applied. This section is rather special in that it is about a particular awareness—the awareness of self as context.

Although more will be said about context in the next chapter, it is important to note at this juncture that conceiving of one's self as a context is truly liberating. Realizing this enables one to communicate it to one's clients with the impact of personal experience. The leverage step here is the shift of expansion or liberation as a single event to expansion as an ongoing process.

The point conceptually is a simple one. Experientially, it is profound. It is simply this. You are not an object. Life does not happen to you. You possess objects, and events may happen to them. But you are not an object. Your life proceeds *through* you. Experience occurs *within* you. There is no more basic frame of reference or container than you. You can recontextualize events because you are the context for the recontextualization procedure itself. Current operational contexts occur at the present time, within you. Past contexts are in your memory and can be reactivated by you or not. Future contexts are yet to be created by you.

Very little else can be said about this awareness. Conceptually, it is a simple idea. Experientially, it is profound. There is no victim. There is no perpetrator. Events occur within a physical universe of space and time. The relevant physical universe, that is to say, your world, your reality, takes place within the context of your Self.

From the standpoint of the clinician, it is important to be practical. As philosophical or as metaphysical as the above may seem, it is highly practical if applied. With the awareness of self as context for all phenomena, the implied "maximum flexibility" is infinite. If you are the context for your entire experience of life, there are no inherent limits to choice and option. You are only limited by what you have already created and by what sets you are currently maintaining.

This limitation does not "happen to you." If you are the container of your life, you are the container of those limitations. It then becomes an issue of deletion, revision, or creation to provide yourself with whatever freedom is necessary to disengage from the given set of circumstances.

Although the most profound of the operational elements presented in this chapter, awareness of self as context is the least directly applicable. This is due to its very nature. It is not intended to be directly applicable. It is more intended to be something of an atmosphere to pervade the work. It becomes useful when it is between the lines rather than when it is overtly and explicitly communicated. For the mystic it speaks for itself. For the pragmatist it can be considered an operational stance.

CHAPTER

# 5

# CONTEXT

Although the subject of context could be understood primarily as a philosophical issue, it is being discussed here for its therapeutic implications. The distinctions between the levels of content, process, and context are well known. Understanding these distinctions is critical to the utilization of these concepts in psychotherapy.

"Content" refers to subject matter. If we were referring to a telephone book, the content would be the names, addresses, and telephone numbers. If we were referring to a person's life, the content would be the events, including physical objects and the circumstances surrounding them. Anything physical, including one's body, is subsumed under the rubric "content." An operational rule of thumb would be if you can directly sense it (see, feel, hear, taste, smell), it is content.

"Process" cannot be directly sensed, but it can be inferred or deduced. Process is powerful; it moves the content. For example, the apple falls from the tree as a result of the gravitational attraction between the earth and the apple. The *process* of gravitational attraction moves the *content* (apple/earth). Its invisibility notwithstanding, process is detectable by its effects in space, through time.

Usually psychotherapy and a substantial segment of psychological theory reside at these two levels, content and process. Content in psychotherapy signifies the details, circumstances, feelings, emotions, thoughts, and symptoms that the client presents. When such items have been treated and the therapy has been successful, the same class of items are used to measure success. How does the person feel? What are the positive new life circumstances?

Process in the psychotherapeutic setting connotes the powerful forces and systems that move such life experiences and circumstances. They are inferred and deduced from the patterning of the "content" through time.

The following caricature may be helpful. A hypothetical client, a 28-year-old single woman named Jennifer, has the presenting problem of fearing that she will never marry. She has just ended her most recent affair with a man named Bill, who is 58 years old, married, and the father of three children. Jennifer's history reveals that her previous lover, John, was 55 years old, married, and the father of two children. Before John, Jennifer was involved with Stephen, who was 57 years old and married. Ichiro, the lover just before Stephen, was 58 years old, married, and the father of two children.

Consciously, Jennifer is convinced that there is no connection among these four men. Bill was English. John was a Texan. Steve was Canadian. Ichiro was Japanese. They had four totally different personalities and lived in four totally different life-styles.

Let us say the psychotherapist in this hypothetical instance was analytically oriented. The therapist would immediately deduce that a common denominator involved older, married men, with or without children. The working hypothesis would be that this is obviously unresolved oedipal material, and the client has been acting out the desire for her father coupled with a defense against it, resulting in multiple such affairs and never marrying.

The therapist holds the oedipal material in relation to those life events as one holds the process of gravitational attraction to the falling of an apple.

With respect to efficacy, one moves up an order of magnitude to operate on a level of process rather than on a level of content. The client herself had tried, unsuccessfully, to find satisfaction by changing content, that is, new lovers with totally different interests and cultural backgrounds. As therapists, however, we know that when an effective change is made on the level of process, positive results finally begin to emerge. The expression of these results appears in the content.

For example, on the process level the therapist assists the client in resolving the oedipal issues and in moving forward in life. The therapist knows that success has been achieved on this level, not by the brilliance of the therapeutic interaction, but ultimately by the change witnessed in the content over time. Several months later the client reports that she is involved with an available man and, a few years later, the therapist is invited to the wedding.

If we wish to move up another order of magnitude from the level of process, we need to consider the following: If "content" is moved by "process," then what moves, shapes, or causes "process"? Operations at that level would surely demonstrate great leverage, that is, maximum result for minimum intervention. "Context" refers to that level.

Unfortunately for the purposes of understanding through the written word, the farther one gets from content, the more abstract one gets. Since process is outside the domain of sensory experience, discussions of that level are certainly abstract enough. The level of context is at the next order of magnitude of abstraction.

Writing on this level usually gives the impression of being mystical and unscientific. The truth is that this is actually an artifact of language, attempting to describe an entity greater than itself. Words are content. They are combined in a process: language and communication. The wellspring from which this process, the very process of communication itself, arises is difficult to describe by the class of entities that arose from it, namely, language.

The reader should be reminded that we are discussing aspects of the nature of human experience. Therefore, nothing that is presented here, from content up to context, is alien to the reader. Artifacts of description and language are nothing more than artifacts. An example of this from everyday experience would be the difficulty one has in describing a pleasurable event, a meal, the experience of a good swim, and so on to an interested listener. It never sounds quite the way it actually felt, but that in no way attenuates the way it felt. It is simply the nature of the relationship between language and experience. The subject of context is introduced when one considers that which *contains* language and experience.

Therefore, in view of the preceding discussion, it will be far easier to deal with the issue of context by means of illustration, analogy, or example, rather than use an inadequate process, such as direct description. There is an abundance of analogs of context in the everyday world. These would ordinarily be referred to as the "setting," "atmosphere," or "stage."

Consider the following example with respect to "setting." We have just finished constructing a brand-new resort hotel. It is totally empty—no guests, no personnel. We enter the resort complex and examine two "settings." The first setting is an Olympic-sized swimming pool surrounded by beach chairs, tables with umbrellas, and a fully equipped bar. The second setting is an elegantly furnished dining room with a fully equipped kitchen, romantic lighting, and tasteful decor.

We have chartered three airplanes to bring in our hotel staff. No one is missing. Everyone is on the plane: maids, cooks, bartenders, lifeguards, and management. The staff arrives at the gates of the resort complex en masse.

It is quite easy to understand how the "setting" will *directly* determine the subsequent processes that unfold as the hotel organizes to receive guests. The simple existence of the swimming pool setting functions as a causal agent in affecting management decisions that direct lifeguards to that place. The kitchen crew is sent to the kitchen.

The word "context" is being used here in contradistinction to "setting" in that it refers to something within human experience, though not necessarily something physical. A more direct example of context in the above situation might be akin to the state of mind of the hotel developer, years before, that produced the thought "I will build a resort hotel." Let me emphasize that context here is the state of mind that produced the thought, not the thought itself. The thought can be argued with, disagreed with, and even defeated. I am referring to an *absolute* state of mind, or role-state, or state of being that might be *translated* into a thought or action. It is that most intangible state of being, "resort-hotel-producer," that results in the necessary processes to shape the content.

A context results from an act of creation and is not physical. It is the experiential setting in which processes develop, in which processes are expendable, and to which the processes conform. Finally, these processes move the content, which in our case refers to the "daily life" that we live.

The reader is now referred to the introduction of this book where it is strongly asserted that the field of transformational psychotherapy is within a field of mental *health* rather than mental illness. It now becomes clear that the reference is to a context. In a context of mental *illness* the processes that practitioners can invent for purposes of cure and use for purposes of diagnosing illness are absolutely limited. These processes can also be understood as being produced by, or being caused by, this context. Changing the context to *health* expands the limits of the set, resulting in processes beyond those related to illness to include processes related to *both* illness and health.

Unequivocally, a change in context is a *profound* shift in a mental frame of reference. I am always impressed with how innocuous that phrase sounds in contrast to the reality of its impact. It is rather like describing a stampede of elephants as "mammals in motion," or a hydrogen bomb explosion as "matter conversion to energy."

Recalling from the previous chapter that the Self could be regarded as the container for the context of life, one can say that transformation involves the facilitation of the individual's capacity to shift the given context.

Herbert Spiegel has developed a well-known single-session method of hypnotherapy designed to disengage smokers from their habit.[1] In a hypnotic trance the individual is directed through the following three concepts:

1. For my body, smoking is a poison.
2. I need my body in order to live.
3. I owe my body this respect and protection.

The hypnotist then teaches the client how to induce self-hypnosis and reinforce these three statements.

What seems to be produced by this method is a shift in the context of the relationship between self and body. Essentially it is a shift from irresponsibility to responsibility. The person emerges with a new context as "responsible keeper of the body." From that new context appropriate processes naturally seem to ensue among those for whom this is a successful method. They discover changes in gustatory experience. Their thoughts about cigarettes totally shift. Their desires increase *beyond* areas related to abstinence for tobacco. Some people begin to eat healthier foods. Others become athletic.

The hypnotist is not required to give process instructions at all. The client seems to "spontaneously" create them to fit the situation. Such is the power of context.

Given a context, there is a principle of *appropriateness* such that all that

---

[1]Herbert Spiegel, "Termination of Smoking by a Single Treatment," *Archives of Environmental Health* 20 (1970): 736–742.

resides within that context is shaped by it. People on the whole tend to respond to the given situation or set of circumstances in a manner that fits the set. This does not mean agreement. It could even mean disagreement.

We tend to limit our options to the given set. It is the exception rather than the rule for an individual to utilize inner capability to expand outside of a given set independent of the consensus set.

When context takes a material form directly and becomes a "setting," it can take many shapes. Some are external, such as the swimming pool or the restaurant in the example presented earlier in this chapter. Some are internal, such as a "role" in the psychodramatic sense. Some are interpersonal in the form of relationship. Whatever form it takes, context can be thought of as the single most powerful element in any system.

Consider the following. A man goes to a restaurant for lunch, sits down at the table, and waits for service. The waiter signals that he will be by in just a moment. Ten minutes pass, and the waiter does not give service. Whenever eye contact is made, the waiter continues to indicate that he'll be right over. After 30 minutes go by, the disgruntled patron signals the manager, who indicates that service will be forthcoming promptly. After another 10 minutes, the angry patron leaves the restaurant and goes to another restaurant.

Later that day, at dinner time, the same individual is at home, alone in his living room. He becomes hungry and goes to the kitchen for a snack.

One would consider the two episodes as appropriate behavior at both the restaurant and at home. Let us bring our attention to the setting and the *causal* nature that it has.

In the restaurant, although this man is very hungry, the *thought never occurs* to him to go to the kitchen, where the food actually is. It is not as though he thought of it and rejected the idea as absurd, he *never* thought of it. Forty minutes were spent thinking of many ways to get the waiter's attention, as well as thinking of other restaurants in the area. These are appropriate thoughts in our culture.

Similarly, at home in the living room, the *thought never occurred* to this individual to "leave the apartment and go to another one" if he was not served immediately. It is not as though he had the thought and rejected it. The only thought that occurred to him was to go into his kitchen and get food.

The setting determined the *limits* of his thoughts as well as his actions, resulting in choice available only within the limited set.

It would be appropriate at this point to expand the notion of setting to include an element of personality organization as well. This could be understood as "role." In the role of restaurant patron, process choices are limited to getting service or leaving. In the role of apartment dweller, the choices are limited to going to the kitchen, and so on.

We have so many roles in life that we would consider ourselves multiple personalities if we were not aware of the different roles and were not comfortable in shifting from one to the other. The role of passenger in a taxi is different from the role of driver in a car. Each is complete in its choices and options. Each is a whole. Each is total.

In this sort of work the best frame of reference for "personality" would be that put forth so astutely by Moreno.[2] Essentially the idea is that a personality is a *collection of roles* rather than a single entity with a collection of traits. The former seems to be clinically more observable than the latter. This idea of the personality is analogous to a cluster of grapes. Each grape is a role complete in itself, with its own "skin," so to speak. We create new roles to handle new points in life. We relinquish old ones when they are no longer useful, and at any given point in time we can move from one role into another, and from that into another. The roles of "apartment dweller" and "restaurant patron" were occupied by the same individual on the same day.

The famous line from Shakespeare, "All the world's a stage," makes this point elegantly. We move from stage to stage and from role to role.

Another point can be added to that of Shakespeare. It is true that all the world is a stage. It is also true that there is a backstage.

The true realm of context is backstage.

The clinical applications of this chapter are basically simple and straightforward. It is an extremely powerful move to change a context. It not only liberates, it also causes processes to unfold that support the actualization of the new purpose.

The various ways to shift a context or change a set are innumerable. A number of them can be mentioned. By the process of *inclusion*, an individual can constantly shift the operating set. In other words, as life progresses, when we experience ourselves in polar opposition to an event or a thought, we discontinue the opposition and instead *include* the op-

---

[2]J. L. Moreno, *Who Shall Survive?* (Beacon, NY: Beacon House, Inc., 1953).

posing thought as our own *with* the original position. By including both oppositional positions, there is no choice but to expand the set to contain these two. Speaking allegorically, if we had a lifetime of beliefs heavily invested in the notion of "cold water," and then one day we stumble upon "hot water," and engage in an intense debate on how unconventional the new temperature is, resolution of the conflict is handled by expanding the set. By *including* "hot water" as a viable, or useful, or positive entity, we can delight in the luxury of "hot *and* cold running water."

Semantically, this is the shift from "but" to "and." For example, a person might say the following:

"I want to go to the movies, BUT I must go to work."

"But" sets up the two circumstances as in mutually exclusive sets. By the conversion of "but" to "and" we unify the set and get thus:

"I want to go to the movies, AND I must go to work."

Here we have two entities that no longer are mutually exclusive. Both are desired, namely, to go to the movies and to meet obligations at work. By expanding the set in this manner, the second position translates an irreconcilable conflict into a matter of scheduling and logistics (process issues).

It is a real resolution of the problem when the set is expanded to include enough, when the context is changed. The original "problem" no longer exists. It is not changed into another form. It is not ameliorated. It is dissolved.

This may sound overly simplistic. The fact is it is just that simple *in the realm* in which contextual change occurs.

What is not simple, what involves struggle is the *unfolding* of the new context in the "real" world, the world of content. That world is physical and requires process, through time and space, to shape it.

CHAPTER

# 6

# PERSONAL DEVELOPMENT OF THE THERAPIST

## CONTEXT OF HEALTH

The psychotherapeutic relationship is a context. When relationships are understood from the point of view of context, their limitations and their power are revealed.

When we think of relationship, we usually think in terms of its physical nature, that is, behaviors, appearances, emotions, and feelings. Here it is better to think of relationship as *that which produces* such behaviors, emotions, appearances, and so on. This is just the sort of discussion that was alluded to in the previous chapter, where the entire matter begins to sound mystical and metaphysical. In a sense, it is just that.

When the discourse becomes mystical and metaphysical, if it implies to the reader something beyond everyday human experience, then it is important to take a second look. It happens to be part of ordinary human experience to have one foot in the physical universe and the other in the nonphysical. Even the prosaic task of ordering a meal from a menu involves a multitude of fantasized dishes, followed by placing the order.

One might prefer to substitute the word "fantasy" or "mental" for "metaphysical." However, there is a distinction. The realm indicated by "metaphysical" in this discussion refers to that *from which* fantasies and other mental activity arise.

A role can be considered a context. For example, in the role of "good parent" in a setting where the child is present, processes unfold and are created or repeated, manifesting changes within the content (appearances, behavior, emotions, etc.) that we commonly refer to as the "relationship."

It would be better for our purposes to apprehend "relationship" in its nonphysical aspect, that is, as the coaction of complementary roles, rather than the behavioral expression of these roles at any given point in time. It is this very coaction that both limits and determines the range within which the variability of process will emerge.

Since we are interested in the therapist–client relationship, a moment spent on the personal development of the therapist would be useful.

As long as the healing arts have been a part of our culture, there has always been an emphasis on the development of the healer. ("Physician heal thyself.") In the field of psychotherapy it has been a requirement of most of the better training programs, or at the very least strongly recommended, that the therapist undergo a complete psychotherapy in order to treat clients.

When the operational context shifts from mental illness to mental health, the traditional concept of "psychotherapy" is not sufficient to meet the needs of the practitioner. The context of illness as stated earlier has limits, namely, when the pathology is gone the process is essentially over. In a context of health, when the pathology is gone a specific process begins, namely, that of health. This realm, health, has no known limits. The implication is one of *ongoing* development and expansion.

To provide such a context of expansion within the professional relationship requires the continued development and expansion of the therapist. This is so, interestingly enough, not for the value of the new realms into which expansion proceeds, but for the very atmosphere of *continued expansion*. The client is not required to develop or expand into the same realms into which the practitioner expands. What is required, however, is the *context* of continued expansion. If the context of personal expansion within the therapist ceases, the cessation becomes the therapist's contribution to the coaction. The contextual message is "There is a limit to human evolution and expansion."

The reader may be struck with the importance of this limitation and wonder whether there might be an ethical question in a mental *health* context. Let me hasten to add that my purpose is not to imply that it is a breach of ethics when the therapist arrives at a point of personal satisfaction in life and chooses to rest there for a time without continuing to develop and expand. It is my purpose, however, to consider the fabric of the client–therapist relationship, particularly during the existential encounter in the office setting. That encounter must have a constant open door to ongoing expansion. Even if one chooses, within the context of continued expansion, to remain in place, this choice can and must be respected as legitimate. Consider the following.

During the nineteenth century in the United States, the western frontier was expanding to the Pacific Ocean. Not all of the pioneers were determined to settle in California, however. Many people left wagon trains to settle in a multitude of places between the east and west coasts. Their choosing to stop was nevertheless *within the framework* of an expanding frontier, making it a free choice, existentially. In other words, "to stop here or to continue on" is a choice *within* the set of "the expanding frontier." Within a fixed frontier, on the other hand, the choice to go further is not available.

Therefore, it is not necessary that the therapist continue to expand and uproot what might be a satisfying position. All that is required is the *context* of expansion itself.

This is easier said than done. It is the rare training program indeed that communicates this frame of reference to its students on a level deeper than simply acknowledging it as a good idea. This is not to fault the existing systems. It is simply the nature of the times. In the terms we have just been using, it is the nature of the prevailing paradigm or context.

It is absolutely within the power of the individual to change a paradigm. What makes a new paradigm prevail, ultimately, is the phenomenon of a large number of *individuals* shifting the paradigm within themselves. Therefore, all that is necessary to create the appropriate atmosphere for personal expansion in the office of the practitioner is for the given practitioner to choose to create the necessary context as an individual.

A number of activities can be suggested along these lines to assist one along this path.

## LEARN NEW TECHNIQUES

The activity of learning new techniques is being proposed with a certain very sophisticated "tongue in cheek." The idea is not to clutter up your practitioner's toolbox with an overflowing assortment of gadgets. Your objective is to experience what having alternative methods does to you as an individual.

When a person has a multiplicity of methods to achieve a given goal, the effect is on two levels. One, of course, is on the level of greater success in goal achievement. The second level is the rewarding personal experience of such expanded efficacy. The ability to have a variety of means to an end produces an absolute increase in efficacy.

Erickson has said that there is no such thing as "resistance." There are only inflexible hypnotists. This is an intriguing operational position and, on the whole, a clinically verifiable one. As one expands in proficiency in a multitude of methods, there just seem to be fewer resistant patients. But more than that, such methodological proficiency enhances the therapist's inner sense of continued expansion, a necessary context for transformational therapy.

Once you have developed a taste for variety of method, it becomes increasingly convincing that one's own personal development can be a major barrier to positive options in almost any setting.

## PERSONAL PSYCHOTHERAPY

Not very much need be said about personal psychotherapy to the professional reader of this volume. The only specific emphasis that I would make here would be the following.

If the psychotherapy is intended to increase efficacy as a psychotherapist as well as to enhance personal development, the choice should be to use a therapist who is also an effective teacher of psychotherapy. The modality of therapy chosen should also contain the area of development professionally as well as personally indicated. Various modalities should be experienced.

From the standpoint of the practitioner of transformational processes that would employ the kinds of powerful techniques mentioned earlier, it would be useful to experience the following modalities oneself. These are presented not for their therapeutic considerations and applicability to given "symptoms," an inappropriate discussion for this volume, but for their utility in the training of the practitioner for this work.

Psychoanalysis, in addition to its therapeutic value, gives clinicians a fluency and rapport with their own unconscious material. In the setting of a classical analysis, the emphasis will usually be on a discovery of pathology and the liberation from it. The by-product, which is what I am emphasizing, will be a comfort in conversing with one's own unconscious mind and a respect for its contents as well as its power. This "by-product" will serve as a useful resource in working with others.

Group therapy experience is highly useful in discovering one's own interactional aspects and in being able to be both inside and outside interactional process.

Psychodrama is one of the single most effective modalities for experiencing the interaction between metaphysical and physical processes. Before your very eyes you have the opportunity to witness dramatic changes simply by the shifting of roles. Entire contextual worlds transform by relatively simple techniques. By the use of auxiliary egos (group members that stand in for significant others), one can actually step outside as well as inside the drama of one's life.

Because it is so powerful, psychodrama has attracted many types of individuals, not all of whom are skilled psychotherapists. As a result, the American Society of Group Psychotherapy and Psychodrama established an examining board to maintain high standards in the profession. This is a relatively new development, but a significant one for newcomers to the field. Psychodrama trainers should, at the very least, be those who are recognized by the board.

With respect to hypnosis, it is advisable that practitioners in this field learn to do *self*-hypnosis. This skill is easily learned; training workshops and appropriate trainers can be found through the Society for Clinical and Experimental Hypnosis and the American Society of Clinical Hypnosis.

There is really no substitute for personal experience in the above modalities.

## EXPANSION BEYOND THERAPY

The problem of expansion beyond therapy would be easily solved if this were India, China, or Japan. In the religious cultural traditions of these countries expansion beyond the "normal" is the rule rather than the exception. In our culture you have to look around a bit for proper guidance in this area.

In the wake of the human potential movement in the United States, one can find a curious mix of legitimate programs right next door to the more "unsavory" types. There are a few guidelines that can assist one in finding a suitable path. The first is that the search is internal rather than external. One will not find it "out there." The expansion one is seeking is the expansion of one's experience of one's self. The function of the teacher or "guru" is that of facilitator more than of importer.

Since one's expansion is truly an individual matter, there is no "best" approach. This is the nature of the matter itself rather than some deficiency in curriculum. To prime the pump, so to speak, and get things going in this area, a number of sources can be recommended. There is, of course, Bhagwan Shree Rajneesh.[1] This master has managed to communicate Eastern thought in a clear and understandable form to the American mind in good contemporary English. I would recommend reading anything he has written, as a start.

Patricia Garfield has written some excellent works on dreaming.[2,3] Her works focus on the dreaming process as opening a path to the expansion of one's healthy self, as opposed to the more typical work on dreams in our culture that focus on pathological aspects.

At this stage of the game, many of the "enlightenment" workshops remain controversial. These include est, Arica, and Actualizations, to name a few. As of the date of this writing, est has trained over 250,000 people. These large numbers bring the phenomenon of such trainings away from the fringe and into consideration by serious workers in the field. If one's learning style flourishes under experiential participation, one may consider this route as a start.

For those preferring to start with reading, the books cited above, plus works by Carlos Castaneda,[4] would be a fine beginning.

It really is not necessary to recommend anything further than the above, since, once one becomes involved at that level, further resources and material in the community will present themselves.

The notion of "resources presenting themselves" is not intended to sound mysterious. What is being respected is the fact that beyond a start in this area, next steps are highly individual. In practice, people tend to gravitate toward the appropriate "next step" once started. The experience of finding it is usually that it simply "presented" itself.

---

[1]Bhagwan S. Rajneesh, *The Book of the Secrets* (New York: Harper & Row, 1977).
[2]Patricia Garfield, *Pathway to Ecstasy* (New York: Holt, Rinehart and Winston, 1979).
[3]Patricia Garfield, *Creative Dreaming* (New York: Ballantine Books, 1974).
[4]Carlos Castaneda, *Tales of Power* (New York: Simon and Schuster, 1974).

PART

# II

# TRANSFORMATIONAL PSYCHOTHERAPY

The first part of this book outlined key areas of preparation necessary for effective entry into operations of transformational therapy. This part will deal with issues of this therapy. It cannot be assumed that the reader has achieved mastery in the area of prerequisite skills before beginning to read this part. Therefore, the material presented from this point on will not require proficiency in performance to understand the issues involved. It makes sense, then, to reread the following portions of this book when, at a greater level of skill, the material will seem far more personally relevant than merely intellectually understandable.

The reader who has achieved proficiency in the skills presented earlier can experiment with the principles that follow. The reader who has not yet attained the level of proficiency necessary to personally test what follows can proceed in a two-phase plan. Phase one would emphasize skills and techniques; phase two involves the application of the principles that follow.

I do wish to emphasize, however, that nothing is presented in this part of the book that I have not personally witnessed in my working with patients. The principles presented are a crystallization of work actually done in an outpatient psychotherapy setting.

A recommended approach to this material is to understand it conceptually and test its relevance clinically. How soon that can be done will depend solely on either polishing or learning certain prerequisite skills. Incidentally, if such a preliminary process is found to be necessary, it will likely be found by the clinician to be fascinating, enriching, and rewarding.

As one reads the following sections, it is useful to keep what is relevant and discard what is irrelevant to one's work. The criterion should be clinical applicability. It would be unfortunate to discard a concept as "clinically inapplicable" simply because skills to test it out have not yet been developed. It would be far better to achieve the level of technique necessary to test out a given principle.

It is to be emphasized that this form of psychotherapy is not appropriate for all people at all times in their lives. In Chapter 1 (see Matching Client and Therapy) criteria for selection are outlined.

I have found transformational processes to have three components:

1. The client's map of the world
2. The experiential challenge and enrichment
3. The new map

They can be sequenced or interwoven. They will be presented here as a sequence for purposes of clarity.

CHAPTER

# 7

# THE CLIENT'S MAP OF THE WORLD

One might rightfully wonder about the term "map of the world." Why not simply say the client's world? It takes only a moment of reflection to realize that what we normally refer to as "our world," experientially speaking, is literally the world *that we experience*. The sky, trees, cars, all of our everyday world, in fact the specific items that these words refer to (sky, trees, cars), are represented in our experience by our sensory systems. Therefore, when we say "car," and it refers to that object that we see (visual) that has the rumble of that engine (auditory) and that certain feel (kinesthetic) when we drive it, it is known to us by this sensory representation.

When we normally use the word "world" or "reality," we usually mean this sensory representation. This representation is created and perceived by means of the sensory mechanisms of the brain and spinal cord. It is an obvious fact, as obvious as saying that the television set produces its picture by means of its circuitry.

The interesting thing is that we do not *ordinarily* think of it in that manner. Holography has become quite popular these days. It is now technically possible to produce a three-dimensional picture, suspended in space, that even captures elements of time so that viewing the picture from one side shows the three-dimensional object in a different moment than viewing the picture from another perspective.

It is rather unusual for an individual to recognize that at this very moment what is being witnessed visually is also a hologram. The page of this book that you are reading and the very room in which you are sitting is a hologram made by your nervous system. Think of it for a moment. It is a three-dimensional picture, and, if you are fortunate enough not to be color blind, it is in full, living color.

It has depth. Given a moment of thought, you realize that there is no place in the visual system in which the *actual* world around us is contacted in depth. Each of the two eyes focus a single image of the presenting scene upside down on the back of the retina. Each of those images is flat, *not* three-dimensional. The only visual contact we have with the world is a flat image, in fact, two of them. As it is well known, for these images to be perceived in the form that we ultimately see them it is necessary to have this "flat" information processed through the cerebral cortex, in particular, those areas in the occipital region. Those two flat images on the back of the eyes are immediately translated into electrical impulses via nerve transmission to the multiple circuits in the brain. The final product of looking at this page, in fact, the thing you call "the page," is the computer printout of all this information. The minor discrepancies between the two flat images are computed into an experiential "printout" in depth.

None of the above is new information to the trained professional, yet why does it always seem somewhat surprising? It has to do with the fact that we do not operate as though the "world in which we live" is a product of our nervous system. We operate as though that representation *is* the world that it is representing.

Of course, we have no choice. To do otherwise would be foolish. Our very survival depends on that operating principle. If one is crossing a street and sees a car coming in dangerously close, prudence would dictate protecting oneself, even if one has the inner knowledge that the visual experience of the car is being created by the occipital cortex from a mass of data coming in from the physical universe. All bands of the electromagnetic spectrum are in contact with the body, but only those relevant to our particular species is being printed out. It makes sense, then, if you see the car coming, to get out of the way. It is the representation of the *real* car.

When one is enjoying a motion picture, the least relevant considerations would be those of the projector. It is only when one wishes to change the film that the mechanics become relevant.

Suffice it to say, then, we have no *direct* personal knowledge of the true physical universe. We do have direct personal knowledge of our representation of the physical universe. This is species specific. Dogs, very poor in color vision but very well equipped in the sense of smell, would experience a room as a multitude of smell experiences far more sophisticated than those we human beings have, for example, when going into a bakery or food market. A human being in the same room as the dog might not smell anything at all but be absolutely captivated by the colorful decor.

It is not only species specific, but also individually specific. The way one human being represents the world may not be at all the way another human being represents the world. This, of course, raises the question of "consensus reality." When one considers the individuality of human experience, it becomes quite amazing that two people can have a sensible conversation about any topic at all. There is a way to understand the phenomenon of consensus reality pragmatically.

Consider the following illustration. The year is 1904. Automobiles have just arrived on the scene. It is a small town in a rural area, and traffic management has become a problem. We wish to establish some sort of traffic signaling devices and have arrived at the idea of using different colored lights. One color would mean "stop," and another would mean "go."

The department of traffic, having recently become aware of certain developments in the area of neurophysiology, understands that color is not an external phenomenon inherent in the objects of the physical universe. Color is a product of the neurological capacity of the given individual's brain to produce the appropriate experience for that individual. It is the "printout" of the frequency analysis of the electromagnetic spectrum contacting the eyes.

This information has sent the administrators into confusion. After all, if everybody sees traffic lights differently, how can order come out of such chaos? A neurophysiological consultant is called in, who resolves the dilemma with the following demonstration.

Three people are selected from the group: Jones, Smith, and Thompson. A piece of electrical equipment is brought in that measures light in terms of its frequency. Its "color" is not mentioned. The machine is turned on at a certain wavelength of light that is to be chosen for the signal "stop." Then the machine is switched to the other wavelength of light, which is chosen to have cars "go." Jones, Smith, and Thompson are asked to participate one at a time. The wavelength for stop is shown to Mr. Jones, followed by the wavelength for go. For stop, Mr. Jones has a particular visual experience and, for coding purposes he calls it "number one." For go, Mr. Jones has a different visual experience, which he calls "number two." It is now Mr. Smith's turn. For the wavelength stop, Mr. Smith has his visual experience, which he calls "A." For the wavelength go, he has a different visual experience, namely, "B." Finally, it is Mr. Thompson's turn. For the wavelength stop, Mr. Thompson has visual experience "alpha," and for the wavelength go, he has visual experience "beta."

The result of the experiment worries the administration even more. Their worst fears are confirmed. There are now six different experiences for the two traffic lights. The consultant is quick to point out the following.

It is true that there are six different experiences. However, there is *consistency* for *each individual*. In other words, Mr. Jones will always experience No. 1 for the stop signal and always experience No. 2 for the go signal. Similarly, Smith and Thompson will each, in their own world, experience consistently their *own same* experience for the same external stimulus. This enables the consultant to proceed as follows.

Turning to all three gentlemen, he switches on the stop wavelength of light, saying, "Gentlemen, *whatever* you are experiencing, since it is always the same experience for you as individuals, be so kind as to call this experience 'RED'."

Switching on the other wavelength of light, the go signal, he states, "And since you always experience this as different from the first signal, and consistently see it as the same experience each time, then, whatever the experience looks like to you as individuals, simply call it 'GREEN'."

He then tests this. Turning on the stop signal, he says, "What do you see?" and *in unison* the three men, say "RED!" Turning on the go signal, he says, "What do you see?" The unison response is "GREEN!" "Thank you, gentlemen. Stop on the red lights. Go on the green lights." The traffic problem is solved.

This may be an oversimplified illustration of the structure of consensus reality, but it does make the point. The point is an important one. Consensus reality is an illusion. Yet, the illusion works. Our lives depend upon it. There is no better alternative to the illusion in the realm of human group experience. The specific illusion of consensus reality is that we all experience the same thing as a group because we *say* we do.

The next level of illusion is not that of consensus reality, but that of individual "reality." The "printout" produced by the experiencing machinery of our neurological circuitry is what we as individuals ordinarily think of as "reality."

I wish to emphasize that there is "reality" in the physical universe. It simply is not the computer printout that we call reality. That "printout" is our personal *representation of* reality.

Since throughout the course of this volume the emphasis is on the therapeutic relevance of the issues brought forth rather than the philosophical questions, consider the following. When a client enters the office with a "presenting problem" or "chief complaint," it is without exception a complaint located *within* the client's representation of the world. Nobody ever complains about the physical universe. Nobody knows what that is like. Nobody can complain about sound at a frequency greater than 20,000 cycles per second (Hertz) because it is not experienced by human beings. No one complains about anything out there that is in the electromagnetic spectrum below infrared light, or above ultraviolet, because we cannot see it. One person complains about the same opera that another person enjoys. As we all know, one is not right and the other wrong. They are both right, given their experience of the world.

The client's world is a map. It is a representation. It is complete in itself. The most useful operating position in respect to that map is to hold it as the best choice on the part of the given nervous system, considering *all* the factors involved. This was a primary operating principle of Erickson and was a cornerstone for most of his therapeutic strategies.

The therapeutic dilemma is on the client's map. The therapeutic "cure" will be experienced on the client's map. The therapeutic process will involve shifts of the client's map.

Where the therapist's map of the world is identical to the client's, there is potential for a "blind spot." Where the maps differ, the therapist is able to perceive the limitations of the map of the client. In those therapies in which the tactical emphasis is heavily weighted in the utilization of content, this is a significant issue.

On the other hand, there are forms of therapy, noted in much of Erickson's work and the work of others who utilize altered states of consciousness, in which contentless therapy can be performed. In this therapeutic method process instructions are delivered to the unconscious mind.

This method frees therapists from the limitations of their own map and eliminates the difficulty of "blind spots." In view of the above, then, a useful approach is to become profoundly aware of the notion of a client's map, and to orient oneself to its presence. Since it will probably differ significantly from the map of the therapist, the next principle would be to support the client's map totally. This does not mean to agree with it, nor to disagree with it, or even to know its details. To support it means to respect it, to communicate that respect, to take the position (or psychodramatically to "step into" the actual belief) that it is absolutely the best alternative the person has, given the circumstances. If done with assurance and sincerity, this form of acceptance can cement the therapeutic alliance. There will be rapport.

The earlier chapter on rapport considers the matter from a standpoint of substructure rather than of strategy. If the above acceptance of the client's map of the world is truly experienced as such by the therapist, yet the client is not evidencing signs of rapport, there may be a problem in the substructures of communication of rapport.

Since very few of us in the United States are trained to conduct psychotherapy in a "contentless" manner, the following excerpt may prove useful.

The client was a 61-year-old woman who had moved to New York City following her divorce six years before. She presented the following problems. First, she felt very lonely and anticipated this feeling getting worse as she got older. Second, she felt bitter and resentful toward people, especially men, and she saw herself withdrawing from her friends. A complete psychiatric evaluation showed no signs of psychosis or severe depression. From a diagnostic point of view, she was considered to have a mild depressive neurosis.

For the purposes of this discussion, the most significant factor was that the client was quite reluctant to share the details of her life with the therapist. The reasons she gave included the fact that the therapist at the time of this work was at the age of one of her sons, and that she found it difficult communicating about "certain matters" with a young man of that age. Further discussion disclosed that she found it difficult discussing "certain matters" with anybody of any age.

It was obvious that the therapeutic work would involve social, and ultimately sexual, adjustment in order for it to be of any value to her. Given the fact that this therapist had the option of proceeding in a "contentless" manner, a lot of time in the preliminary phase of treatment was saved. In fact, it is questionable whether or not verbal psychotherapy could have occurred at all if an insistence on content would have been made, given the client and the particular therapist involved.

THERAPIST: Okay, I understand the situation, and I can appreciate how difficult things can be for you at this time. But, you know, there's really nobody in the entire planet that can appreciate *exactly* how difficult these past few years have been for you, other than yourself. I mean, isn't that true?

CLIENT: [*some tears beginning to well up in the eyes, yet controlling herself*]: Yes, I think you're absolutely right. How could anybody really know what it feels like?

THERAPIST: Okay, that's why I'd like you to know that there's a very special way to work with this kind of difficulty that allows you to keep your privacy on these matters, and still get some definite help.

CLIENT [*look of disbelief on her face*]: I don't know what you mean.

THERAPIST: Yes, psychotherapy has really come a long way, and it's not always the way you've seen it in the movies and on television. There have been some remarkable advances in recent years that might just be perfect for you. Look, let's be realistic. You really don't want to go into great detail about your private life and certain very personal matters dealing with men, with me, directly. Isn't that correct?

CLIENT [*nodding her head "yes"*]

THERAPIST: Well, obviously, if any change is going to occur in your life for the better, it's going to be done by you anyway. It isn't going to be done by somebody else, therapist or otherwise. Changes are going to occur within you.

CLIENT: Of course.

THERAPIST: All psychotherapy is is a way of communicating to one's own system what the problem is and having one's own system make changes. I mean the therapist doesn't go around living everybody's life for them. Ultimately, whatever goes on in the therapy, the person coming to see the therapist is going to make the changes. Not the therapist.

CLIENT: Right. [*still having a quizzical look on her face*]

THERAPIST: I think it'll be much easier if I give you an example.

CLIENT [*face relaxing*]: That sounds like a good idea.

THERAPIST: Okay, here's an example. I'm going to ask you to think of something, but I don't want you to ever tell me about it. I really want to respect your privacy. Do you understand? I just want you to think about it. I don't want you to tell me about it. Okay?

CLIENT: Okay.

THERAPIST: I want you to think about the situation these days with respect to your social life, particularly with respect to men. And I just want you to think of the best example in your private life, right now, that you would call "evidence" that things are not going so well with men these days.

CLIENT: You mean just think of an example of how I don't have a social life right now?

THERAPIST: Yes. I'm saying let's say you were a lawyer making a case for the prosecution, and you were gathering up evidence that "this is a woman that does not have a social life these days." What would you use as evidence? What kind of a situation or a scene, and in what part of the house, or in what part of the city.

The only difference is, I just don't want you to tell it to me. I want you to have it in your mind. I want to respect your privacy, keep it a secret. Just gather the evidence.

CLIENT [*spontaneously closing her eyes*]: Okay, I'm imagining a situation right now that is perfect.

THERAPIST: You mean, it's just right.

CLIENT: Yeah. [*visibly upset*]

THERAPIST: So if this pattern were no longer in your life, you would say that we would have achieved a good piece of psychotherapy. Is that correct?

CLIENT: Absolutely.

THERAPIST: Okay, just as promised, I don't want you to tell me anything about it. Just give it a code name so that we can talk about it. In other words, you can even give it a number, from one to ten, or a letter of the alphabet, like pattern "A" or pattern "B," or some code name.

CLIENT [*slight smile, but still visibly upset*]: How about just calling it "alone."

THERAPIST: In other words, the code word for this pattern is "alone." Of course that doesn't necessarily mean what the dictionary would mean by "alone." It is simply a code name.

So if I say the words "pattern alone," you know exactly what I mean. Is that correct?

CLIENT: Absolutely.

THERAPIST: Okay. The next part of this process is handled entirely by your unconscious mind. Naturally your unconscious mind knows what "pattern alone" is, it just gave you the memory of it.

CLIENT [*nods head "yes"*]

THERAPIST: Furthermore, your unconscious mind has *within it* the part responsible for "pattern alone." So really all we have to do is establish communication with the part responsible for "pattern alone." That's the part that in order to serve some purpose in the unconscious has this one way of doing it, namely, "pattern alone."

CLIENT [*furrowing of the eyebrows*]

THERAPIST: I know that it's hard to conceive of how "pattern alone" could be serving some positive purpose. Usually purposes in the unconscious, which I sometimes call "intentions," are serving some protective function or safety function or security function. And it's quite possible that sometimes a person might unconsciously be protecting herself from hurt feelings or, I don't know what, by minimizing involvements with other people. The point is the whole matter is unconscious. I don't know what positive reasons are being served by your system in activating a pattern as dissatisfying as "pattern alone." And I'm sure you don't either, because if you knew what purposes are being served, you might want to figure out another way to serve those purposes. Anyway that's what we are about to do at this point.

CLIENT: You mean figure out some other way to serve those purposes?

THERAPIST: Well, in a way, yes. Except you and I are not going to do the figuring out. Let's leave the whole matter to your unconscious. It's very creative and whatever your IQ is, the unconscious IQ is about a million.

At this point, the therapist, with the client's permission, induced a mild trance state in the client, and, when the client was at the appropriate level of trance, suggestions were given regarding ideomotor signals for "yes" and "no."

CLIENT [*in moderate trance state, breathing slowly, minimal movement*]

THERAPIST: All right, I would now like to get into communication with the part responsible for "pattern alone." When I'm in communication with that part, I will get a "yes."

CLIENT [*left eyebrow twitches*]

THERAPIST: Thank you. And what would be a signal for "no"?

CLIENT [*right index finger moves up half an inch*]

THERAPIST: Thank you.

At this point, the therapist continued the process as discussed in the section on Reframing in Chapter 4 of this volume. The session lasted approximately one hour, and the client was scheduled to return to the office in one week.

On the return visit, she was noticeably in a positive state of mind and reported that, over the week, she had spontaneously begun to leave fattening foods out of her everyday meals, and started looking for new clothes. She was wearing makeup that was quite fashionable and appropriate to her age. She also reported that she had started to telephone old friends to get together with them and made arrangements to start visiting.

The rest of the psychotherapy was conducted in this manner. She would come in twice a week. On Mondays we would do reframing on subjects that she preferred not to talk about. On Friday, interestingly enough, she would be willing to discuss some of the subjects that she had been unwilling to talk about on Monday and would report progress in those areas. These Friday sessions were supportive, really the sharing of news. There was no attempt to uncover or interpret. By the end of eight weeks, it was not necessary to continue meetings, since she had achieved enough progress to assume that it would continue. At her request, we discontinued sessions with an agreement that there would be some follow-up conversation in the future.

Follow-up at six months and then again at two years revealed that a continuing process had unfolded. She lost the weight that she wanted to lose and became quite active socially. In fact, whatever criteria I would use to describe a successful psychotherapeutic outcome, I would use to describe the results in this case. The key difference in this case was that the active aspects of the psychotherapeutic intervention were done totally on a contentless basis throughout.

Many points are illustrated by the above example, namely, hypnotic communication, linguistics, the use of reframing, and so on. The emphasis being made in this section of the volume is on the engagement of the client in the client's model of the world, in particular, respect for the client's map. This case demonstrates the sort of efficacy one discovers when one is willing to accept and support the map as it is. The revisions are made on that map. The positive outcomes are also on that map. The therapist in this case simply utilized principles of map revision and creation. More will be said on the revision of the map in the next two chapters.

Nevertheless, it becomes clear that the therapist has a choice in the matter when it comes to initially engaging the map of the client. The choice is between disclosure and nondisclosure of content. Having engaged the client in the client's model of the world and established rapport, motivational factors need to be considered. After all, one's map of the world provides one with great security. Changes in the map need to be handled with caution and prudence. All too frequently prudence and caution are mistaken for "resistance" in psychotherapy, when it comes from the client.

Motivational systems can become the mutual allies of the therapist and client. It is not necessary to employ a separate procedure to induce motivation, as demonstrated in Chapter 4. It can be woven into the interaction, allowing the client's unconscious mind, by transderivational search, to stimulate the client away from inertia and maintenance of the status quo.

Here is one example of the use of transderivational search that has proved to be quite successful: The therapist reminds the clients that the world has changed for them many times in the past when it has been necessary. It is a common experience for all of us to return to the neighborhood or playground of our early childhood, or to a schoolroom that we once were in, to be amazed at how small it seems, how the chairs have shrunk, how the swings in the playground are so small. Well, what happened to the playground? What happened to the schoolroom? Who shrank them? One can point out to clients that their "scale" of size on the internal map was adjusted because of their shifting body size. Instructions can be delivered to the unconscious to make such a shift in the therapeutic context, equating both situations as similar. The similarity is that circumstances in life have changed, and it is necessary to update the system.

## PERSONAL HISTORY

Earlier in this volume, we discussed the use of personal history as part of the diagnostic evaluation of the client. Its function is to provide information, that is, content, as well as to assist in diagnostic considerations regarding the applicability of one therapy or another.

The act of taking a personal history can also be a therapeutic intervention, and on this level we will discuss it here. The client's map of the world is not only spatial, it is also temporal. Personal history is actually part of the map. It serves to locate oneself within the coordinates of space and time. It defines character and personality for clients in varying degrees.

As a means of communication, subliminally, that the map of the world is not the world, it is useful to have the client communicate a *complete* personal history. "Complete" in this sense does not mean excessively detailed. "Complete" means that there is a beginning, a middle, and an end and that it is encapsulated. This enables the client to distinguish "history" from "not history" and distance from personal history itself.

I frequently ask clients to deliver to me a "20-minute version" of their life. I assure them that I know they are intelligent and feeling individuals, that I have noted this in their interaction with me so far. Therefore it is *not necessary* to communicate details in their life with intense feeling, merely to communicate the fact that they have feelings. (Naturally, if feelings arise, they would be understandable.) In other words, during this procedure clients should present their summary life history as though they are speaking about someone else. If a certain item in the history has been traumatic, they should state it as "traumatic," but should not relive the trauma. Conversely, if an item in the past was ecstatically pleasurable, they should indicate it as so, but not relive the ecstasy.

This procedure has the appearance of information gathering. The subliminal effect is disengagement from the temporal map for that moment. The subliminal communication is also the expendability of the map itself.

For some people whose investment in their past is clearly a barrier to needed development in the present, a specific altered-state exercise can be done along the lines of the following.

---

**CASE**

Mr. G., a 58-year-old businessman, delivered a history indicating the lineage of his family back to the Mayflower. The overemphasis of "respectability" by his parents, he felt, led him to the stifling life-style of which he complained. After he delivered the history, he was told that it was routine at this point to do a rather refreshing mental exercise.

He was asked to close his eyes and imagine himself in a theater that had three movie screens. When he could clearly see the screens, he would nod his head. Upon establishment of the theater, he was requested to have "the projectionist" run his entire life on one of the screens from the very beginning through to the time he came to my office, in superfast motion. He was told he had 60 seconds to do that. He was given signals at 30 seconds, 45 seconds, 55 seconds, and finally when the 60 seconds were up.

He was then told that often people wish they had the chance to do life over again. He was going to have this opportunity to do this now. Using his creativity and sense of humor as well as his deepest wishes, he was to allow the projectionist to project an *alternative* life on one of the other screens, one that he wishes he would have had. Further, he was instructed that he would have 60 seconds to do this. He was given the signal to start, and signals at the 30-second, 45-second, 55-second, and finish points.

Having witnessed an "alternative" life, he was then told that, since it is so rare that one is given the opportunity to do something like this, and in the event that he may not have exercised his privilege to the fullest, he was going to be given one more chance to *really* create a totally different history for himself. This would be on the third screen. It didn't matter what birth he chose, what sex, even what species, as long as the story ended with his coming into my office, for whatever reasons. Once again, he was given the signal to start, intermediate signals, and the signal to finish.

After he had stopped laughing, with his eyes closed, he was told that the following would ensue. At the count of three, the projectionist was going to simultaneously run the three films on the three screens, and that he could feel free to glance from one to the other, according to his own whims. He was further informed that it was important for him to pay very close attention, because the projectionist would insert, at random, in the midst of these "lives," cartoons and Laurel and Hardy film clips. After he evidenced much enjoyment of the ensuing show, instructions were given to "the projectionist" to show some of the film upside down, and some of it backward, and finally all three would be running in their usual forward direction.

He was then instructed to let the movies disappear from the three screens, while still visualizing the three screens. Then he was to "thank" each screen individually for permitting him to live in the given life. Following that, he was "thanked" by each screen for permitting them to exist, for clearly, without him, they would not exist. After that procedure, he said a pleasant farewell to all three, for the time being.

He was then told that he was going to be asked a question by me, and that the answer was to be kept secret to himself. The point was not for me to know the answer, but for him to have the experience of noticing whether he even had an answer.

When he got the answer that "came up for him," he would simply signal me nonverbally. He was then presented with the following question.

"Does it *really* matter which one of the three lives was the actual one?" After he signaled me, he was then told to let go of his theater comfortably and reorient himself to the consulting room with his eyes closed, and once fully oriented in that manner, he was to open his eyes.

The client reported a feeling of a "burden having been lifted." A session was scheduled a week later to continue the evaluation. When the client returned a week later, although we engaged in more diagnostic work, the entire first half of the session was filled with reports by the client of a marvelous week spent between the two sessions. For "unexplainable" reasons, he didn't seem to feel as in need of psychotherapy as before, although he was quite motivated to continue in whatever process we were engaged in.

---

It is interesting to note how one can communicate the message that history is part of the map, that it is not the "truth," but an arbitrary and useful personal representation of the truth.

## SIGNIFICANT OTHERS

Another dimension appears in the mapping of one's world, namely, that of interpersonal relationships. The greatest interest lies in the quality of these relationships, as well as the specific people involved. On the interpersonal map the cast of characters defines the boundaries, and the quality of the relationships forms the contours.

As in the case of personal history, the interpersonal world also has two separate realms of interest to us. The first is that of content. This area, for the diagnostician, has its applicability as described earlier in Chapter 1 under the heading Matching Client and Therapy.

The second realm of interest, appropriate to this section of the book, is the exploration of interpersonal relationships as a tactical maneuver. The implied message we wish to deliver to the unconscious is that the constellation of relationships constitutes a piece of the map of the world of the individual. The constellation itself is an option, the very structure of which can be revised. In fact, revision might be advisable if the given constellation is a source of dissatisfaction.

This would imply the need for techniques that encapsulate an entire constellation at once, rather than those that explore in a linear sequential fashion. In this way one can easily separate "constellation" from "not constellation."

An example of such a technique is a sociogram.

Shortly after the delivery of the "20-minute version" of personal history in an initial consultation, a client might be given a sheet of blank paper and a pen and be asked to construct a sociogram. The procedure takes about 20 minutes, 10 of which are the delivery of instructions and the other 10 the process itself. The following is an excerpt from such a session.

---

**CASE**

The client is a 35-year-old married man, father of two girls. He is handed a blank pad of paper and a pen and instructed "not to do anything yet." He is informed that the entire paper represents his personal universe rather than the physical universe. He is told that he is about to make a schematic representation of his relationships. Males will be represented as triangles; females will be represented as circles. He is to place in the center of the page a triangle to represent himself. Around this triangle he will orient the symbols for people that he "experiences," in his life.

It is made clear that this is not the physical universe. Some of the people that he may experience in his life may have physically moved great distances from him in space or in time. Some may be alive, some might not be. Some may even be mythical figures.

It is made clear that this is an internal exploration of the truth. The question is "Who's there?" It is also made clear that this is *not* "Who shall we invite to the party?" If we invite Uncle Dave, we must invite Aunt Sue. He may have taken a bus to the office with 50 other people. They would not appear on such a representative diagram.

There are two distinguishing features for purposes of representation on this diagram: placement and size. He is instructed that these features have no intrinsic meaning. Instead he is to utilize them to express the truth of the relationship. Placement is described as "near and far." Size is described as "large and small." It is totally up to him to utilize these parameters to express the current state of the relationship.

He is further informed that it is a slice of life. It is a current statement. The time frame of the sociogram is the present, whatever "nowadays" means to him.

He is further informed that the process is over when he gets the idea or inner feeling that "That's about it, for now."

The client worked for about five minutes and produced the sociogram below.

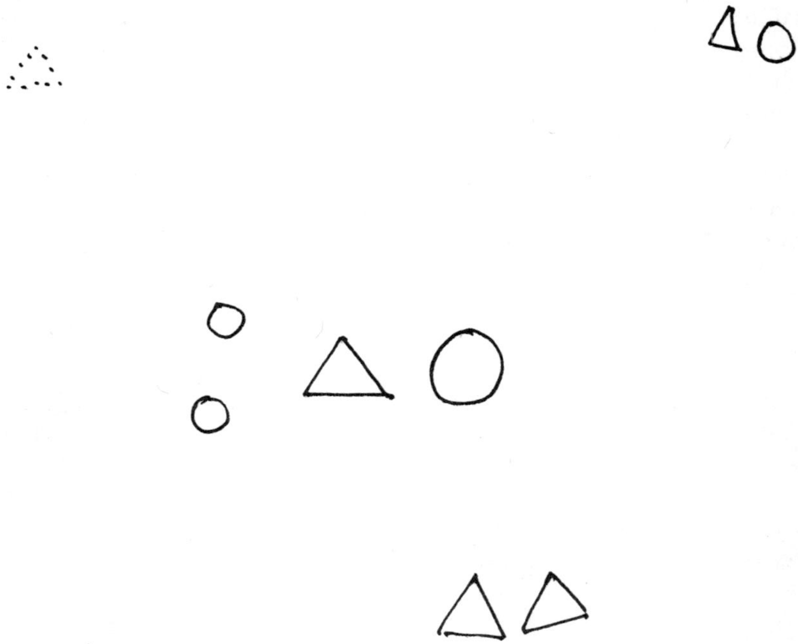

The client was then informed that obviously the therapist has no idea what these triangles and circles represent, and the extent to which he would wish to share information would be greatly appreciated. The client indicated that the circle next to "him" was his wife, and the two smaller circles nearby represented his two daughters, the dotted triangle in the distance was his deceased grandfather, the circle and triangle in the far right were his parents. The two other triangles in the middle of the sociogram were his two friends. The client was then asked, given this overview, whether there was anything about this situation that he might like to change, revise, improve in some way.

---

It is of interest in the above situation that the importance of the grandfather and the two friends never came up in the taking of the personal history. As an information-gathering tool, this type of sociogram, referred to in the psychodramatic literature as a "social atom," is invaluable. Information appears in an initial consultation session in a matter of minutes that would ordinarily take weeks, if not months, of ongoing sessions to emerge.

The sociogram is a marvelous technique and its applications are unlimited. Interestingly enough, the emphasis in this particular section is not on its information-gathering value, but rather on the message that the very structure of the sociogram communicates.

A picture is worth a thousand words. Language is a linear process through time. In contrast, a picture conveys instantaneous understanding of the whole. By the very placement of relationships on a single drawing, the client is confronted with a unit, a gestalt, rather than a multiplicity of detail. Even if the figures are scattered all over the sociogram, the sociogram itself is a *single* sheet of paper. When one holds a sociogram, one is holding a map.

The implications, even through the kinesthetic channels of the hands themselves, are that you can hold *other* things. That which is in the hands can be picked up and put down. One can manipulate within the set, or manipulate sets. It is a profound message to the unconscious. The message can be enhanced by making appropriate statements to the client on this very point.

Moreover, the client can be told that the sociogram itself is a piece of cooperation between the unconscious mind, the conscious mind, and the therapist. It is a form of computer printout of one's relationships, and the unconscious has access to such computer capabilities. Remarks to the effect that the unconscious mind is an ally, the source of great nonlinear thinking, and it is participating in this very process, are not only reassuring but very intriguing to most people. These observations have the additional benefit of indirectly suggesting that future work ought to proceed in a similar positive manner.

There is one additional point. The central figure on the sociogram is a representation of the client. It is very rare in the processes of everyday life that we can have such a perspective of our own placement of significant others. The duality of seeing ourselves represented on paper in the midst of our relationships, while at the same time being seated in a therapist's office looking at such a diagram, is remarkably effective. It communicates subliminally that "All the world's a stage," and that we have deeper choices than we imagined.

Another message communicated is that we are not only the principal character in the play. We are also the producer and the playwright and, perhaps, even more.

## EMPHASIS ON THE NEGATIVE

There is the metaphor about transformation regarding the caterpillar. The caterpillar complains to his friend about the overwhelmingly tiring struggle he has every day to climb the branch and get to the food. This caterpillar is a genius, so he begins to wonder about inventing an elevator or a staircase. Perhaps an escalator might work. The cosmic joke is that, naturally, when he becomes a butterfly, the entire question is irrelevant.

Although the client may have a capacity for contextual change similar to the caterpillar's change in physical structure, the client might not be aware of this. In fact, it is the rule rather than the exception that clients are unaware of their capacity to transform the experience of their lives. They, like the metaphorical caterpillar, can only think of what is wrong with their life, how difficult it is, how negative. To speak to the caterpillar about wings, when the caterpillar has been a worm his entire life, is not only inappropriate, but also unfair, even if it is the truth.

The caterpillar's map of the world is that of a caterpillar, not that of a butterfly. The client comes in with emphasis on the negative. Sometimes it is useful, tactically, to join the client in this emphasis. The therapist can afford to have an optimistic frame of reference, since the therapist knows about metamorphosis and the capacity for contextual change. Yet, initially, it is foolish to emphasize anything other than what the client brings into the office.

It is therefore very useful to get an accurate list of the client's multiple chief complaints. In the earlier sections of this book, the function would be for accurate information gathering. Here, however, the function is to have a *complete* list, a beginning, a middle, and an end. This enables the client to experience an implication of *beyond* the list itself. It distinguishes "list of complaints" from "*not* list of complaints." There is more to life than those negative items.

It is sometimes useful to be observed writing down the list on a pad as it is being recited, constantly interjecting phrases to the client such as, "Are you sure there's nothing else that bothers you?"

Occasionally, a client will look you in the face and say, "Isn't that enough?" It is a positive atmosphere when both therapist and client are residing outside the boundaries of the list itself. This is accomplished simply by exhausting the list. Strangely enough, items rarely go beyond 10 or 15. This experience can be uniquely liberating, since many people experience their difficulties as endless. The experience of "endless" difficulties is a function of placing oneself within one's map as a character in the play, rather than in the position implicit in this interaction, namely, the directorial or playwright position. These roles are offstage, if not outside the theater entirely.

## DEVALUING WISHES

The devaluation of wishes is a tricky point technically. It is really a matter of strategic sequencing. In other words, when should the therapist place a value on the client's wishes, and when should the therapist devalue them?

Offstage, so to speak, we are operating in a positive frame of reference. Onstage, in the initial phase of a transformational interaction, optimism may be the least appropriate position, since it is not on the client's map.

Consider the caterpillar once again. Prior to transformation into the butterfly, the caterpillar's wishes are appropriate to the existing set. Given that the mode of transportation is travel on the ground by crawling, ingenuity and creativity produce ideas such as the elevator, the escalator, and so on. The best solution, in fact, the one that will actually occur, does not occur in the caterpillar mentality. Wishes or even possible "solutions," *at this stage of the game*, are merely natural by-products of the existing limited set.

Let us clarify this even further. The therapist is not being advised to overtly devalue the wishes of the client. Naturally, the client's map of the world is to be respected, and this map includes its wishes. The therapist is advised to devalue these wishes within his or her own mind. These wishes may be quite appealing; after all, it is possible that they might even find correspondence in the therapist's map of the world.

When transformational processes occur, there is a fundamental shift of the set. At this point wishes or goals are reevaluated. As in the story of the butterfly, the emergence of wings not only solves the presenting problem, but changes the map of the world radically. One needs problem-solving capabilities (the "wish" system) available for the new arena, not tied up in better forms of ground transportation.

## ALIGN WITH RESISTANCE

The subject of resistance deserves special commentary here, since it is such a noticeable issue, particularly in the early phases of the process. From a tactical point of view, Erickson's contributions are immeasurable. His principle, "There is no such thing as resistance; there is only an inflexible therapist," is a marvelous guideline.

In this section it is worthwhile to emphasize the underlying features that render Erickson's guideline appropriate. In particular, if value judgment is removed from the question of resistance, then it could be understood as the voice of structure itself. If one wants a drink of water, a liquid, it is necessary to have a vessel to contain it. The whole function of the glass or the cup is to provide the necessary resistance to the natural property of the liquid to flow. The usefulness of the receptacle is obvious: it permits us to carry liquids around. The vessel says "stop" to the liquid.

When one encounters resistance, it can be thought of as coming up against the edges of a structure. When you align with the resistance, support it, and agree with it, then it is no longer pointed at you, to say the very least. Taken one step further, aligning with resistance is a communication to the client's unconscious. It is a message that clearly says the therapist has a respect for structure and is not interested in a chaotic expansion of the personality.

In transformational work, form is better than chaos. We are striving for alternative form. Form expresses the underlying context. Upon the revision of context (e.g., the caterpillar: a ground creature to an airborne creature) new revised forms should emerge (wings). They will have their own structure and, of course, their own "resistance." We therapists, in our work, have no argument with resistance. We require it and we respect it. It holds the structure together.

Furthermore, the emergence of resistance is a message to the therapist from the client's unconscious, indicating that the work of the given moment is a threat to structure. The skillful therapist at this point, supported by technique combined with the awareness of these metalevels of change, receives the message and shifts appropriately.

## SUMMARY

A complete transformational process can be said to have three parts. First, the engagement of the client's map of the world, second, an experiential challenge with concomitant enrichment, and third, the emergence of a new map.

This chapter has dealt with the engagement of the client's map. The next chapter will focus on loosening the connection to that map to enable a responsible substantive revision to come in as the "new map."

It must be emphasized that what will be challenged is the client's map. What will not be challenged is the legitimacy of using a map in order to navigate in the physical universe. To disengage oneself from one's map of the world and not come up with an alternative map is irresponsible, to say the least. One was better off with the original map, dissatisfying though it was. For a proper appreciation of this idea, the following chapter needs to be regarded in that light. A study of disengagement from the original map is incomplete without the information presented in the final chapter, namely, the creation of the new map.

CHAPTER

# 8

# THE EXPERIENTIAL CHALLENGE AND ENRICHMENT

At this point, we are well into the process. We have engaged the client in the client's map of the world. We have done this in a manner that has enabled distance to be introduced between the client and the client's map. This naturally sets the stage for the next step in the process. Keeping in mind that we are striving toward the establishment of a new, more satisfying map, the notion of invalidating or casting doubt on the existing map becomes a responsible process. I stress this point because some of what is proposed or suggested in this chapter involves methods that at times may be disorienting or confusing to the client. In fact, what is orientation if not the mapping of time, place, and person?

Without a proper perspective, this invalidation just seems to be destructive. When medical students encounter surgery for the first time, they might be impressed by the fact that the doctor is intentionally cutting someone. It is dramatic. The necessary factor is the proper perspective, the proper frame of reference. Medical students must understand experientially as well as cognitively that *in order to* assist the patient they are obliged to employ procedures that would seem to be destructive in and of themselves, but in the context of methodical therapeutic intervention these same procedures contribute to healing, and are therefore necessary and desirable.

Similarly, some of the procedures and strategies outlined below throw a person off balance. At the proper moment and in the hands of the skilled and ethical practitioner, this is precisely what is necessary and desirable.

## PRIMACY OF EXPERIENCE OVER COGNITION

There is the expression, "Seeing is believing." If you wish, you can add the other sensory modalities as well. Hearing is believing. Feeling is believing. Smelling or tasting is believing. Certainly, if all senses are taken into account and found to be in agreement on a certain event, that event is considered to be a fact. If you see these pages in front of you, feel their texture, hear the sound they make as they rustle against your fingers, you can be pretty certain that they are actually there.

This is useful information if you wish to assist others to change their map of the world. The principle is simple. If you can give someone an experience in sensory terms (visual, kinesthetic, etc.) that absolutely does not belong in their world as they know it, you have performed a profound intervention. It is a challenge to the very epistemology. If the intervention is made in the form of experience, and not in the form of verbal argument, the challenge is irrefutable.

The foundation of the original map was experience. It becomes very difficult indeed to maintain the original map when conflicting items are presented, using the same measure of validity.

If done effectively, the client moves from a position of "knowing the way the world is and disliking it" to a new position of "not knowing the way the world is." This naturally casts doubt on any conclusions drawn from the original "knowledge" of the world, such as life being dissatisfying.

Of course, as stated earlier, this would not be an end point. It is clearly an interim state, namely, "not knowing what the world is." The demand for a new view of the world becomes intense at that point. Therefore, this is the time the new view is offered or created.

Following is a clinical example in which a certain hypnotherapeutic process for the alleviation of pain, commonly used for headache, is utilized as the experiential challenge to the old map. This particular method is reputed to be ancient. The details follow, but, in general, the client is asked to concentrate on the experience of the headache itself, rather than to run from it. Moreover, the client is asked to develop the experience by adding other characteristics to it. When effective, the headache disappears. With this in mind, note the following excerpt.

---

**CASE**

The client, a 32-year-old single woman, had multiple areas of dissatisfaction in her life. Although basically bright and resourceful, she was unhappy in the areas of career and social life. By the time she had come to this therapist, she had experienced other therapies in which she had gained insight and some movement in her life. However, fundamentally, she seemed "destined to live out a dissatisfying story." It became clear during the initial sessions that fundamental belief systems about her capabilities were negative and, although dissatisfying, they formed part of the integral fabric of her map of the world. She also complained of chronic, intermittent headaches.

During the course of one of the early meetings, she indicated that she was having one of the headaches at that time. She was asked by the therapist, in a rather innocuous manner, as to whether she would like to "disappear" the headache. She responded that she would, and asked for an aspirin. The therapist replied that he knew about aspirin, but was serious about the idea of "disappearing" it. She responded that she did not understand.

"Excellent," said the therapist. He then proceeded to offer the patient an "experiment." She seemed intrigued and curious. She decided to proceed.

THERAPIST: Would you uncross your legs and close your eyes.

CLIENT [*uncrosses legs. Closes eyes and shifts position in the chair*]

THERAPIST: Okay. What are you experiencing in your head right now?

CLIENT: The headache.

THERAPIST: Let's get more specific. What you call "headache" is really a specific sensation. Is it a pressure, is it a tingling, is it a burning? What is it specifically?

CLIENT: It is a pressure.

THERAPIST: Good. The key to this method is to be specific, accurate. It is not often that one takes a direct look at a headache. That's what makes this unusual. Take a good look at this headache. Where is it?

CLIENT: In my head.

THERAPIST: Be a bit more specific. In fact, be very specific. Where in your head? Next to your scalp? Near your ear? Where?

CLIENT: In the front, near my left eye.

THERAPIST: Good. Now get very specific. If you had a ruler, how far in from your left eye? How far in from the left side of your head, and how far down from the top? Measure where it's located and measure how large the pressure is.

CLIENT: Oh, it's a couple of inches or so . . .

THERAPIST: Not a "couple of inches or so." Use an imaginary ruler. Get specific. Is it 2¼ inches, 2⅛ inches on your ruler? [*Therapist's voice becoming more assertive and demanding of high standards*]

CLIENT: Okay, it is 2¼ inches from the left.

THERAPIST [*interrupting*]: What shape does this pressure have? Is it round? Is it triangular? What is the shape?

CLIENT: It is sort of egg-shaped.

THERAPIST: What are the dimensions of the egg?

CLIENT: It is about an inch long and ¾ of an inch wide, at the widest point.

THERAPIST: Good. You've got the right idea. Now where is this egg-shape of an inch long and ¾ of an inch wide located?

CLIENT: An inch and a quarter behind my left eye, two inches down from my scalp and half an inch in from the left side of my head.

THERAPIST: Excellent. Now you're being specific. If it had a color, what color would it have?

CLIENT [*pause*]: A reddish-brown.

THERAPIST: Good. And if it held water, how much water would it hold?

CLIENT: Approximately two tablespoons.

THERAPIST: And what are you experiencing in your head right now?

CLIENT: The headache.

THERAPIST: How big is it now?

CLIENT: Oh, that's interesting. It still is egg-shaped, but it's smaller. It's half an inch long and about a quarter of an inch wide.

THERAPIST: And what color is it?

CLIENT: That's interesting too. It's now blue.

THERAPIST: And if it held water, how much water would it hold?

CLIENT: About a teaspoon.

THERAPIST: Fine. And what are you experiencing in your head right now?

CLIENT: Interesting. It's not exactly a pressure, it's a "presence" of some kind.

THERAPIST: Good. What shape does it have?

CLIENT: Still egg-shaped of some kind, approximately. . . . It's smaller. About a quarter of an inch long and an eighth of an inch wide.

THERAPIST: Good. And what color is it now?

CLIENT: Yellow. That's interesting.

THERAPIST: And if it held water, how much water would it hold *now?*

CLIENT: About two drops.

THERAPIST: Good. And what are you experiencing now in your head?

CLIENT [*silence. Scanning eye movements are visibly occurring under the lids*]: Nothing, I guess.

THERAPIST: Nothing?

CLIENT: Not really. Yes. Nothing right now.

THERAPIST: Good. Open your eyes.

CLIENT [*opens eyes, staring somewhat blankly into space*]

THERAPIST [*in a normal conversational tone*] Well, that's what it feels like to disappear a headache.

CLIENT [*in some sort of state of wonderment; a quiet voice*]: That's really something.

THERAPIST Yes. I know. Headaches are not supposed to go away just like that.

CLIENT [*head nodding "yes"*]

THERAPIST: Yes. There was a time also when I thought I knew exactly the way this world worked. I continue to be amazed by all the things I don't know about. You know what I mean?

CLIENT [*thoughtful; nodding "yes"*]

THERAPIST: Maybe we can get rid of a few other things in your life that you don't like either. Maybe not by the same sort of process, but maybe by other kinds of methods.

CLIENT: Well, headaches are one thing, but a love life is something else entirely.

THERAPIST: Maybe you'd like an aspirin.

CLIENT [*laughing*]: Okay, what do you have up your sleeve for "love life"?

---

Here is another one of those circumstances in which an interaction can be analyzed and understood from many points of view: linguistics, pacing and leading, hypnosis, sensory modalities, to name but a few. For our purposes, the emphasis is on a totally different level. We simply wish to notice the use of an epistemological challenge that is irrefutable. By utilizing the principle of the primacy of experience over cognition, the therapist presents the client with an experience that is not supposed to happen. Yet, it does happen, and when it does, it is undeniable. It occurs in the client's experience (personal reality). It occurs in the presence of another (consensus reality). Finally, it does not belong in her map of the world. She attempts to place it on her old map by considering it an exception rather than the rule. The therapist counters by implying the cost of such a maneuver. By once again offering her an "aspirin" he signifies that he acknowledges her statement as a return to the old map, and he is willing to return to it also. She appreciates that this closes the door to the new and the promising, and opts for keeping the door open.

On a deeper level it is communicated that the entire map of the world might be incorrect if something actually exists that is not supposed to exist, in this instance, the ability to "disappear" a headache.

The seeds of distrust of the old map are planted. The tenacity to it, nevertheless, is indicative of the fundamental health of this individual. Unless we have another map, we had better not throw out the old one. After all, it is the only one we have, and it has served for survival over these many years, even if it is dissatisfying.

There are innumerable ways to offer epistemological challenges. The field of hypnosis offers many possibilities in this area. By the utilization of hypnotic phenomena, the therapist can offer experiences to the client that "should not happen" in the realm of ordinary experience. Arm levitation, automatic movements, and so on can be utilized in this manner.

Hypnosis was presented earlier as a form of powerful communication and a method for large increments of change with minimal effort. In this chapter it is being utilized in a different manner, that is, as a medium to present phenomena that would not ordinarily be experienced by the client. Then the skill is to leverage that moment into a generalization about the client's map of the world. Depending upon the therapist's style and the appropriateness of the intervention, such a move can range from a gentle comment that all is not known about the world, to a forceful criticism of the client's arrogance in thinking that he or she knows anything at all worth knowing. The therapist does what is necessary to assist the individual to let go of the old map and thirst for a new one.

For example, a therapist is working with a client whose arm is cataleptic as a result of suggestion. The client truly experiences an inability to move the arm. Utilizing the moment for an epistemological challenge, the therapist might say, "Do you usually sit in a chair in that manner? Is this the way you normally experience your arm? Isn't that interesting? Isn't that *really* interesting?" Then when the therapist gives a posthypnotic signal that releases the arm, and it comes back to normal immediately, the therapist might continue,

> Now look at that. Your arm is back. Is it every day that your arm is paralyzed and then cured? And I'm sure you think *I* caused that because I am a hypnotist. Don't you realize that if I spoke to the wall, it wouldn't do that with its arm? If I spoke to a dog or a cat, it wouldn't do that. If I spoke to any machine, a car, a telephone, it couldn't do that. Don't you realize we're speaking about your potential to release control of your entire left arm so that it's paralyzed and then your talent or capacity to regain such control, based on an external word. . . . You have powers and capabilities totally untapped at this point in your life.

The moment of epistemological challenge can certainly be one of the most dramatic points in any psychotherapy. It is a point of high receptivity and potential for learning. It is a moment of great opportunity for therapist and client.

## ENRICHMENT

If handled supportively, and with respect for the depth of this process, the moment following or surrounding an effective epistemological challenge can be the opening of great personal enrichment for the client. There is a regaining of cognitive innocence unparalleled except by that of childhood. The psychoanalytic literature might refer to this as regression in the service of the ego. I do not think that that is a helpful construct. It seems far from regression. It could be analogous to the "landing" in a staircase. After climbing in one system for a number of steps, one achieves an area of neutrality, the landing. One shifts one's direction and position before encountering the new set of steps. It differs from childhood in that there is an innocence combined *with* adult resources. There is an "I don't know anything" coupled with an "I *know* that I don't know." There is the combination of intelligence, capability of functioning in the moment, personal mechanisms of survival, and absolute knowledge of the present by means of sensory experience. There is a curious mixture of knowing and not knowing.

One of the best examples would be some individuals lost, on a beautiful morning, in a sunlit forest surrounded by flowers. They are absolutely certain that they are lost. They are absolutely certain that they "do not know where they are." On the other hand, they absolutely do know where they are. They are in front of that tree. They are next to those flowers. They are listening to those birds. They are seeing those clouds. They are absolutely standing exactly where they are. There is no doubt that they know where they are. The dilemma is they do not know where that specific, definite place is *in relation to* other places that they know about.

Being lost means that one *does* know where one is; one simply does not know where that is in relation to the rest of the world.

If only one had a map.

Nevertheless, if an immediate assessment of the given situation is that it is a safe one, a benevolent one, a positive one, then even without a map, one can temporarily make oneself at home. This is good for the system. It has a cleansing effect. Wonderment emerges. A true desire for discovery surfaces. There is, on a deeper level, an inner awareness of untapped posibility in life. There is an atmosphere beyond optimism. It is a direct experience of being given a "second chance" in life. In fact, there is the presentation of an entire new realm of "second chances." One might even ask, "Where have I been all my life?"

It is a refreshing state of mind. Even though one may be totally lost, the heart still beats, the lungs still breathe. In fact, the world seems to go along quite well all by itself, without any need for one's understanding of its magnificence in order for it to function.

Delightful as this may be, after a period of time, which varies from individual to individual, there emerges a demand for new organizing principles.

CHAPTER

# 9

# THE NEW MAP

The client is ready for a new map of the world. Here is where it is crucial that the therapist be aware that a map is just that. It is a map. It is a construct. It is a representation. It is not the world.

When using a map properly, one pretends that it is not a construct. One pretends that it is the world. Consider, for example, the experience of driving a car and pulling aside to check the road map. The speaker always uses the verb to be when addressing the map. One points to the red line on the map saying, "Okay. Here we *are*, and we have to go over there (pointing to another part of the map), so that we ought to *be* there in a couple of hours."

The reality is it is not true that you *are* on that red line. You *are* in that car, at the side of the road, not on a red line. The red line is simply a representation of where you are. As we stated earlier, the experience of the car itself is a representation of where you truly are. You can never directly experience where you truly are. You can only experience your representation of where you truly are.

The best you can do is to experience one map or another. Life is experienced through and on such representations. There is no need to fret about this, since the representations are revisable. Some people hate spinach when they are children and love it when adults. I assure you, the spinach has not changed one iota.

The client is ready for a new map. It is important for the therapist to realize that this thirst for a new map on the part of the client is really a desire for a whole new world. The client has moved from

1. I know the way the world is, and I don't like it.

To

2. I have no idea as to how the world is, but it sure is interesting.

To

3. Okay. Please tell me the way the world is.

At this point, the client needs assistance to recognize that nobody knows the way the world is; that it is just a matter of having a better map; that this is good news, not bad news; that from this point forward, life will be one of continued expansion and growth into unknown territories.

The analogy of the explorer is very useful. If the year is 1492, and one wishes to leave the known map of the world, travel from Europe, and venture beyond the horizon toward the west in search of India, one has to be willing to change the map and revise it.

Let us fictionalize some of history and say that the explorer lands on the East coast of what will be the United States. He calls it India. He gets off his boat and makes base camp. Everything is recognizable. It is a beach. He knows what a beach is. He needs firewood. He sees trees. He knows what they are. Everything is recognizable.

Then, by surprise, from behind the trees, appear natives, and the chief seems to be wearing a feathered headdress. The explorer, anticipating "Indians" as he knows them to be, expects to see the turban headdress. It is a mistake at that point for him to conclude that the Hindus are having a party, or have gone crazy, or have changed their style. At that point he must be ready to revise his map. Perhaps this is not India.

The collapse of the previous understanding of the world, namely, that this was India, does not necessarily herald a psychotic break. Instead, it is (and actually was) the opening of brand-new, unparalleled opportunity. An entire continent was discovered, complete with heretofore untapped resources.

Simple as it may seem, I know of no better metaphor for operating at this point than that of competent explorers. They know they are not going for a "new map." They are going for *continuing* revisions of maps, continuing explorations, and continuing discovery.

It is important for the therapist to hold these principles clearly in mind when clients are tossed off balance by some of the new experiences.

There are other concepts to keep in mind, for example, some of the tools of the explorer. One is the trust of sensory experience itself. When an astronaut lands on the moon, or a fifteenth century explorer disembarks on a new continent, he cannot rely on the findings of previous workers. He can only rely on the present findings. That is not a disadvantage. Being equipped with eyes that see, ears that hear, and a body that feels, one has all that one needs.

This reliance on sensory experience allows us to overlay the navigational matrix of belief systems. Belief systems hold things together. When sensory experience challenges the belief system, we allow the belief system to lose the battle, and we create a new belief system. Belief systems are expendable to the explorer. The explorer is discovering and learning, not dictating and suppressing.

There are innumerable methods that we can use to create a better map. One very effective technique is to communicate the principles of map revision to the unconscious, rather than communicating content of some new map. The following excerpt illustrates the use of this technique in a psychotherapeutic session.

In this case it was elected to use direct communication to the unconscious with the client in an appropriate altered state of consciousness. The instructions to the unconscious mind are totally contentless. No details of the client's life are mentioned in these instructions. Instead, instructions are delivered to the unconscious on the level of form. On that level the instructions are very specific and very detailed.

The excerpt will be broken into sections. It is important to keep in mind that it is from a transcript of a single, continuous session. This particular transcript was chosen because it represents the direct utilization of the principles of creating a new map without the distraction of matters of content.

I hasten to add that it is absolutely not necessary to use a "contentless" method to achieve the desired therapeutic end. Although content can be utilized very profitably in this communication, the fact is that content tends to be distracting. Strange as it may seem, in this work operating in a contentless manner is excellent for the newcomer to the field. When proficiency has been achieved on the level of contentless therapy, enabling the practitioner to be fluent in the matter of form, then interspersal of content is more elegant and engaging. With full awareness of a sequence of appropriate form, content will add humanity, depth, and richness rather than "distraction."

In order to make some sense out of the following transcript, the reader needs to know a few details about the actual therapy situation. The scene takes place in the office of the psychotherapist. The client is a 35-year-old man. Intentionally, for purposes cited above, nothing more will be said about the content of his case, other than to indicate that his problems were on a characterological level, involving many areas of his life.

The initial taking of history and psychiatric evaluation, qualifying the client as appropriate, had been done prior to this session. This particular session was the fourth in the series.

The point of relating this excerpt is to give the reader a realistic sense of one procedural option that can revise the world map of the client. This particular session lasted approximately five hours; however, the part of the session specifically involved in the revision of the map of the world, took only 45 minutes. The earlier portions of the session dealt with the issues described in the previous two chapters.

Rather than leap directly into the transcript at this point, which would be like coming into the middle of a movie or a play, some more orientation would be helpful. The client had been in the office for approximately three hours. We had reviewed the presenting problem and engaged in dialogue and interaction that included many epistemological challenges, and the client was quite ready for change.

In this session it was elected to use the reframing model of Bandler and Grinder, as described in Chapter 4 as a "core" procedure. In addition, certain modifications of my own were employed. One modification in particular was that, rather than having the client identify a single pattern that he wished to change, a special collection of many patterns was made.

It is strongly recommended that the reader refer to Chapter 4 as many times as necessary during the reading of the following work in order to reorient to the six-step reframing model. The first step involves identifying the pattern that the client wishes to change and assigning a letter or number to it.

In revising the client's map of the world, the modification was to identify not only one or even many patterns, but to identify *everything* that the client wished to change. This may seem to be asking a bit too much. There is a collection process that can be employed, however. I found it convenient to ask clients to draw a circle on a piece of paper or on a blackboard and, internally, to identify a pattern that they wish to change. Once they have identified the pattern in their mind's eye, they indicate this with a symbol in the circle, usually an X. Then I ask them to identify another pattern that they wish to change, and when they get it in their mind's eye, to place another X in the circle. In this manner, clients may recall many patterns in their life, and place an equivalent number of Xs within the boundary of the circle.

I lead clients through an inventory, covering many areas of life, asking for patterns that they wish to change. Without revealing content to the therapist, clients might respond by simply placing more Xs in a circle; these have great meaning to the client, and remain undescribed to the therapist.

The inventory ends with my asking if there is "anything else in the world" that the client wishes to change, and, when those Xs have been exhausted, there is nothing else that the client wishes to change in the entire world.

We then assign a *single* letter or number to stand for the entire collection in the circle, and that becomes the "pattern" that we run through the reframing model. It can be considered a megapattern.

We do not stop at this point. This megapattern is held within a context in the client's unconscious. By means of certain hypnotherapeutic exploratory techniques, we locate the "negative" context that produces or causes this "negative" pattern, then, the context producing that context. Ultimately, the polarity of the contexts shifts from negative to neutral to positive, until we find a positive context enclosing both the megapattern and its neutral-to-negative contexts.

Each negative context, when discovered, is entered as a new X in the circle. The entry of Xs stops at the point that we encounter a context positive enough for the client to be willing to base the rest of his or her life on it.

At that moment the client assigns a final code name to the collection. We agree that that collection represents everything in the world that this client wishes to change, *including the negative contexts that produced it*. Further, that everything outside the circle represents what the client does not wish to change, what he wishes to keep. It takes approximately one hour to make this collection.

In the excerpt that follows, the client has given the collection the code name "C3." A hypnotic trance was then induced. The client achieved a relatively deep state of relaxation, seated in a chair, and the induction had been comfortable and slow. The excerpt begins at a point approximately 20 minutes into the hypnotic trance. The therapist begins to communicate instructions regarding the revision of the map of the world to the unconscious.

Map revision is accomplished by means of the provision of new patterns by a "creative part." In Chapter 4, in the section on Reframing, the "creative part" is defined in rather simple terms. A considerable part of the following excerpt is devoted to the definition of "creative part." Delivered to the client while he is in a sufficiently deep hypnotic trance state, these instructions provide the foundation for constructive transformation.

The very structure of the "creative part" described during the instructions to the unconscious is actually a communication of the criteria for the new map of the world.

Hypnotic communication is frequently filled with poor grammar. This is linguistically necessary at times for technical reasons.[1] This may make reading the following excerpt a bit difficult.

The reader should bear in mind that the following words excerpted from hypnotic communication are all delivered by the therapist. This excerpt will suffice to illustrate one way a revision of the map of the world is done.

> . . . and when the part responsible has distinguished between its pattern and its intention there is a creative part.
>
> . . . there is a creative part deep in the well of creativity in the unconscious . . .

The following version of the "creative part" shows a great deal added to the original model of Bandler and Grinder. Substructures within it are defined and enriched to bring emphasis to aesthetics as well as adequacy. Personal satisfaction is emphasized.

> . . . deep in the unconscious there is a creative part that can create brand-new, satisfying, "satisfying" means satisfying to the highest standards of the conscious mind with respect to aliveness . . .

---

[1]R. Bandler and J. Grinder, *Patterns of the Hypnotic Techniques of Milton H. Erickson, M.D.*, vol. 1 (Cupertino, CA: Meta Publications, 1975).

A strategy is presented to abstract a sequence of experience to define and embellish "satisfying." The first member of the sequence is "aliveness."

> . . . and what is "aliveness"? The unconscious mind can scan through memories of oneself or of others as to what aliveness is, and locate two or three exquisite examples of aliveness, and discover what aliveness is by separating the recipe for aliveness from the circumstances of aliveness. What is the recipe for the experience of aliveness? It's not the circumstances. In other words, what does the world *look* like with aliveness and *feel* like with aliveness and *smell* like with aliveness, and *feel* like with aliveness and *smell* and *taste* and *sound* like with aliveness? What is aliveness? The unconscious mind can locate the recipe for aliveness, the structure of aliveness itself. And if it's not in oneself and it's in others, the unconscious mind can reverse roles with the other and from that position, looking out with *those* eyes and feeling with *that* body what is the appearance of the world with aliveness, and how does it feel, smell, taste and sound like with aliveness, and in this manner locate what aliveness is . . .
>
> . . . so there's a creative part that can create new, satisfying, satisfying with respect to aliveness, and well-being . . .

A second criterion is proposed for "satisfying": Well-being.

> . . . what is "well-being"? And the unconscious can locate two or three examples in oneself or in others of "well-being" and using a similar process extract out the recipe for well-being. What does the world look, feel, smell, taste, and sound like with well-being? What is "well being"? . . .
>
> . . . there's a creative part that can create new, satisfying, satisfying with respect to the highest standards of the conscious mind, with respect to aliveness, well-being, full self-expression . . .

A third criterion for "satisfying" is proposed: Full self-expression.

> . . . what is full self-expression? Not 99%. What's *full* self-expression? The unconscious mind can locate examples of full self-expression, in the past, to extract out and extract the recipe, the juices of full self-expression. What does it look, feel, smell, taste, sound like in full self-expression? And not only full self-expression . . .

A fourth criterion: Health.

> . . . but also health, and health not only in the sense of not sick, but health in the sense of the body supports the self and the self supports the body. And the body is available for the purposes in life. And . . .

A fifth criterion: Love.

> . . . and love, and love not only in the sense of sexual or romantic love, but a person can love a place or a thing or a sound. And one way you can love a place or a thing or a person is with *full acceptance*. In other words, it's all right exactly the way it is . . .
>
> . . . and it's all right exactly the way it is *not* . . .
>
> . . . and it's all right if it changes. So a person can love something like a plant as strange as a cactus because it's all right that it's a cactus, perfectly all right that it's a cactus . . .
>
> . . . and it's all right that it's not a rose . . .
>
> . . . and it's all right if it changes. It's all right if it turns into a butterfly. But it doesn't have to turn into a butterfly because it's perfectly all right if it's a cactus . . .

This definition of love has the added advantage of an internal loop in the system. As clients become more accepting of their *own* change as a result of this process, they will have an increase of love for *themselves*, and self-esteem will increase.

> . . . love in *that* sense of the word. So there's a creative part that can create new, satisfying, satisfying to the highest standards of the conscious mind with respect to aliveness, well being, full self-expression, health, love . . .

A sixth criterion: Personal ethics.

> . . . and high personal ethics, personal code of ethics appropriate at this place and time and age and joy . . .

A seventh criterion: Joy.

> . . . and what is joy? The unconscious knows how to locate what joy is . . .

An eighth criterion: Pleasure.

> . . . and pleasure. What's meant by pleasure?

A ninth criterion: Giving.

> . . . and giving . . .

A tenth criterion: Belonging.

> . . . and in relation to the planet itself . . . it *is* my planet. I belong here. It *is* part of me. I am part of it . . .

An eleventh criterion: "Other" such standards.

> . . . and other such high standards of the conscious mind. And it's these standards that the word "satisfying" means . . .
>
> . . . so there's a creative part that can create "new," "satisfying," satisfying to those high standards of the conscious mind, "adequate". . .

On the same order of "new" and "satisfying," the criterion of "adequate" is presented. It is the most basic of all standards.

> . . . adequate means "it works in the world." It works in the real world. *At least as well as the previous pattern*. It works in the physical universe. It works in the mind. It works in the body. It works. It works in the real world. It works "out there." It is immediately implementable. That's what "adequate" means . . .
>
> . . . so there's a creative part that can create new, satisfying, adequate alternative patterns for *any* intention whatsoever.

Having established the necessary "creative part" a revision of the world map can be made as in step 4 of the reframing process of Bandler and Grinder (see Chapter 4). Actually, *several* viable maps are generated:

> . . . the part responsible for pattern C3 having now, distinguished between its pattern and its intention will, now, get in communication with that creative part and communicate its intention to it . . .
>
> . . . now, when the creative part receives that intention it simply creates three, four, five, or six *new, satisfying, adequate,* alternative patterns for that intention; and communicates these new patterns . . . [*pause*] . . . to the part responsible for pattern C3 . . .

As in step 5 of the reframing model, the part responsible ratifies the new patterns.

> . . . and when the part responsible for pattern C3 receives these *new* patterns . . . [*pause*] . . . it takes responsibility for these new patterns, gladly, particularly after scanning them and discovering that they do, in fact, serve its intention at least as well as pattern C3 ever did. The creative part simply creates according to what it receives, from the part responsible. So the part responsible can gladly agree to use these new patterns *first*, in all the old situations . . .
>
> . . . when the part responsible for pattern C3 has received its new, satisfying, adequate, alternative patterns, *now*, for its intention, it simply takes

responsibility for these new patterns and agrees to use them first, realizing that now it has a choice in the matter . . .

. . . that having been done . . .

We are now ready for step 6 of the reframing process: the "ecological check."

. . . [*pause*] . . . it is extremely important . . . the unconscious, now, scans the entire system . . . and when I say entire, I mean the entire system, to discover is there any part anyplace, anywhere whatsoever that objects to these changes? . . .

. . . all systems are to be scanned. There is no system not scanned. To discover: is there any part, anyplace, anywhere, whatsoever, that objects to these changes? A part objecting is not negative or objectionable . . . any part, large or small . . . any part that objects is just a part that needs help. Now if there are no objections that's fine, that simply means that this would be the end of the process. However, this is also an opportunity for the unconscious to learn this process for use in the future as well as now . . . and so, if at this point in the process there are objections, this is the procedure to be followed . . .

. . . the unconscious scans the entire system and gets in communication with the part that's objecting. In the event that there are more than one part that's objecting the unconscious gets in communication with all parts that are objecting at once . . . has all of the parts that are objecting distinguish exquisitely between their patterns and their intentions . . . [*pause*] . . . that having been done, there's the creative part that can create new, satisfying, adequate, alternative patterns for any intention whatsoever . . .

. . . all parts that object, get in communication with that creative part and communicate their intentions to it. The creative part, upon receipt, simply creates three, four, five, or six new, satisfying, adequate, alternative patterns for those intentions, and communicates these new patterns to the parts that are objecting, respectively, and when the parts that are objecting receive the new patterns for their intentions, they simply take responsibility for these new patterns in addition to their previous patterns, agreeing to use the new patterns first. So that they don't have to object anymore . . .

. . . after these new patterns have been installed and the parts don't have to object anymore . . . after the installation of new patterns, the unconscious scans again for objections to those new patterns. And gets in communication with all parts that are objecting, has those parts distinguish between their patterns and their intentions, has those parts communicate to the creative part their intentions and has the creative part communicate back the new patterns, which the parts objecting take responsibility for, agreeing to use them first, keeping their previous patterns in reserve . . .

. . . following that installation the scan goes out again for objections. All parts that object are gotten in communication with and assisted so that they don't have to object anymore, in a similar manner . . .

. . . after that installation another scan goes out for objections. Another installation occurs, another scan for objections, another installation *until there are no more objections* . . .

As in the notion of TOTE, presented in Chapter 4, criteria are presented for exiting the system.

. . . and the unconscious mind knows that the process is over *when* the part responsible for pattern C3 has agreed to use its new patterns first and there are no objections anywhere in the system . . .

An intrapsychic signaling system between unconscious and conscious is established:

. . . and the conscious mind will know that the process is over when the unconscious mind signals it in one of the following ways . . . either the index finger and thumb of the left hand will close together by honest, spontaneous, unconscious movements without any attempt on the part of the conscious mind to make those movements . . . or, the index finger and thumb of the right hand will close together and squeeze, by honest, spontaneous, unconscious movements without any attempt on the part of the conscious mind to move these fingers . . .

. . . or the eyelids will flutter open all by themselves . . .

. . . if it's the fingers signaling the conscious mind, then the conscious mind will reorient to this time and space, to this room, be seeing, feeling, hearing, and smelling this space, and then opening the eyes will be voluntary . . .

. . . if the signal is the fluttering open of the eyelids, by honest, spontaneous, unconscious movement, then, orientation to the room will be immediate and complete . . .

Posthypnotic instructions are given that presuppose the completion of the process. The affect of "well-being" is another signal of completion:

. . . but whether its the fingers or the eyelids, when the eyes are open it's an opportunity for the unconscious mind to give the conscious mind that particular powerful and profound and comfortable and convincing experience

> of well-being that's appropriate to a person whose system, for the moment, is conflict-free . . . meaning that there are no objections anywhere . . .

Here a new step, "step 7," is added to the reframing process. It deals with the experience in the future of the process of emergence, in life, of the new patterns. The awareness of actualization of new patterns should be *after*, rather than during, the occurrence:

> . . . in the future, as these new patterns begin to emerge in life and manifest themselves in the physical universe as real patterns, it's preferable that the conscious mind be *not* aware during the emergence of the new patterns, that they are in fact "new" patterns. Such awareness would interfere with the spontaneity of the emergence of the new pattern. Therefore, it would be far better that when the new patterns emerge, the conscious mind simply be participating in the new pattern, but *immediately thereafter*, at the nearest possible resting point and at the most appropriate point for retrospective reflection on what's occurred, it would be ideal for the conscious mind to then become, suddenly, by surprise, *totally aware* that the new patterns that just emerged were, in fact, "new." And, second, that they were performed with the fluency and with the ease, as though they had been rehearsed and performed many repeated times in the past . . .

Although the models of "conscious" and "unconscious" serve a purpose during the intervention, in the context of participation in life later on, they could be experienced, unfortunately, as dividing oneself into two "parts." Here, the posthypnotic instructions for unity over divisiveness are introduced. Furthermore, instructions are given that pride and responsibility can be taken for the action of the *unconscious*.

> . . . and the conscious mind will be aware that these new patterns were also new patterns that were produced by the person's own unconscious mind, not by "coincidence" or "the weather," and that, in addition, not only were they produced by the unconscious, but the awareness that the unconscious mind is *not* "somebody else." The unconscious mind is simply the vast pool of resources and talents of this individual that are just outside of conscious awareness . . . so that it needn't be experienced as something separate, but in fact a result of one's own talent, a talent that one was not even aware that one had . . . and so that, in addition to being aware that the new pattern that just emerged was in fact *new* and produced by one's own unconscious, in other words, by one's self, but in fact there can also be the experience of pride and self-esteem in the new pattern, in the understanding and knowledge

> of having done it all by oneself with as much great ease and simplicity that all of the everyday miracles of life are produced with such ease and simplicity, without the slightest idea as to how one does it . . .

Having introduced the elements of unity over "parts," the move to autonomy and self-sufficiency are introduced. Instructions to proceed without the therapist are delivered:

> . . . in addition, the unconscious mind can utilize this entire process from beginning to end any time it appears that one is in a totally stuck position in life. "Stuck" means where there are truly no good choices anywhere whatsoever, and after exhausting all systems of possible moves to make in life, the unconscious mind can recall this process . . . because this is a process in which a person can *create* choice where there was no choice, create alternatives where there are no alternatives . . . and the unconscious can choose to use this process . . .
>
> . . . this process can be used at night during dreams, using the dream process to allow the person to sleep rather comfortably, to enjoy the rather interesting or possibly amusing dreams, while at the same time permitting the person to complete the process and awaken in the morning or when sleep is ordinarily over, feeling refreshed and good since all objections have been handled . . .
>
> . . . this process can also be used by the unconscious during the daytime as long as there is enough consciousness to take care of what needs to be done, since the unconscious mind can do this process rather rapidly . . .
>
> . . . now, in a little while I'm going to say the words, "I'm getting out of the way now." After I say those words I'm going to be silent for 30 seconds, because I know that the unconscious mind can complete this process in under 30 seconds, but for reasons that I don't know about the unconscious mind might choose to complete this process in a minute, or a minute and a half, or two minutes, or two and a half minutes, or three minutes, or *less* . . .
>
> . . . so in the event that the unconscious mind has chosen to wait to complete this process until now . . .
>
> . . . I'm getting out of the way, *now*. [*pause for 30 seconds*] . . . now that's just 30 seconds. And I'm wondering if you're wondering just what the signal's going to be. I have no idea. Will it be this one? Or will it be that one? . . . and it's important that your unconscious mind thoroughly does this process and handles all objections. There's nothing for you to do. There's no need to move. There's no need to talk . . . and yet, you can have another one of those experiences that's pleasant and comfortable and rather enjoyable . . . just the experience of simply not knowing which signal it's going to be . . .

To assist the intellect after coming out of this trance, instructions are delivered to direct the conscious mind to the appropriate arena for speculation:

> . . . and your unconscious mind can also understand a very profound use of your intelligence, your conscious intelligence later on in the unfolding of this process, rather than wasting a lot of time in doubting, rumination, and skepticism. The intelligence can be utilized in true scientific application of intelligence, which is, later on, your intelligence can be used in true scientific observation and discovery in real behavior in the real world as to what new behavior you might in fact witness that you're doing, rather than spending time with intelligence attempting to find reassurance in discussion over what might happen. And so . . .

CLIENT [*eyelids flutter open, facial tone returns, a large smile appears on the face, more color appears in the face, the eyelids are fully open, and there is absolute alertness and awareness in the appearance*]

THERAPIST: Hi. Arthur Phillips, 74th Street. Hello.
[*pushing the therapist's chair back behind the desk and walking over to the original chair of the first consultation and history taking session while continuing to speak to the client. This results in the original arrangement of the room on a day the client first arrived*]
How do you feel?

I am sure that the above transcript was difficult to read. This is quite understandable. It is a by-product of the very nature of the subject matter. In hypnotic communication, as indicated earlier, it is necessary to employ linguistic patterns that are highly ungrammatical. It is the very nature of "embedded commands" and other sorts of structures that they be phrased in a manner that makes excellent hypnotic impact but very difficult reading.

Nevertheless, it has been my clinical experience that following such a session it is the rule rather than the exception that satisfying transformational change is manifested in most individuals over the ensuing months. Although the psychological revision is complete at the time of the session, the manifestation in the physical universe may not be complete for some time.

There reaches a point, somewhere in the short-term future after this process, when enough has been manifested to allow client and therapist to be convinced that the process was in fact quite successful.

This sets the stage for a new level of personal development. Clients then become impressed not only with the results of the process, but also with their capacity to change their own life that such a process implies. The interest shifts from the specific dilemmas of life and their solutions to the ability to make significant changes. It elevates the client's concerns.

## RESPONSIBILITY

At this point the client is capable of experiencing responsibility in the creation of his or her own world. A deep recognition that one is at the bottom of it, at the source of the experience of life, is the exact opposite of a burden. It is a release. It is a liberation. It is freedom. When clients have enough time experiencing their power to create the world, they then can experience that they are no better and no worse than other human beings. Human beings are rather magnificent creatures, and the experience of the ability to transform the quality of life is, per se, a demonstration of magnificence. It is from this sort of experience that true compassion emerges. Compassion, in this sense, does not refer to charity, the gift from a superior to an inferior. Compassion is the appreciation of another's magnificence, and the unique dilemma of being human.

In this kind of therapy, the client is clearly empowered with the realization of his or her own health and strength. There is an absolute emphasis on autonomy, particularly at this stage. Any attempt to engage the therapist in a dependency relationship is thwarted, and the necessary experiences are delivered to the client to make autonomy sensible.

This establishes the therapist in the role of guide, rather than healer. The therapist is considered as an equal, simply more experienced than the client. The guide welcomes the client as a fellow explorer into the unknown. There is a certain esprit de corps.

Subsequent sessions continue to emphasize that life includes negative as well as positive elements, and that hard times are not necessarily signs of psychopathology. Life can be considered a game. It has its penalties. It has its glories. One does have the power, however, to change games and create new ones. A true transformational process ends with continuing expansion and development. It is not a "new high." The full range of human emotion is included.

There remains the principle of constant inclusion and expansion. Nothing is said to be off limits. When something new occurs in life, it is included, even at the risk of shattering the previous epistemology. The new map that then emerges is richer and far more worthy of one's time.

## CENTEREDNESS

It is difficult to define centeredness, yet it is one of the most important concepts in transformational work. Stated simply, centeredness is the ability to remain appropriate at all times.

It is an important idea, in view of the realms explored in this sort of work. After all, if one is changing belief systems as though they were articles of clothing, or dissolving one's very map of the world, it is easy to imagine going mentally astray.

To be centered is to be balanced on both levels, with one foot in the practical and everyday world, and the other in the metaphysical, and certainly not losing one's balance. It can be said that one can have the freedom to dream the most incredible dreams because one continues to have the power to wake up.

It can also be said that one can continue to wake up because one has the power to dream.

# INDEX

## L



## M



## N



## O



## P